THE LOVE BOOK

an anthology

Blue Cedar Press
Wichita, Kansas

THE LOVE BOOK: an anthology

Copyright © Blue Cedar Press

June 2024

10 9 8 7 6 5 4 3 2 1

First Edition

https: www.bluecedarpress.com

Editors: Gretchen Eick and Laura Tillem

Cover photograph by Michael Quackenbush, used with permission.

Cover and interior: Gina Laiso, Integrita Productions, Inc.

Judges: Denise Low (poetry); Paris Cunningham (short story); Ted Ayers (memoir)

ISBN: 9781958728260 (paperback)

ISBN: 9781958728277 (ebook)

Library of Congress Control Number (LCCN): 2024936217

No Artificial Intelligence was used in the writing of this book.

INTRODUCTION

Many things in life give us pleasure and joy, but what lasts the longest and is most redemptive is love.

The poems, short stories, and memoir pieces in this volume are the result of a contest. Blue Cedar Press invited entries about the many forms of love. Here are the independent judges' choices of the pieces worthy of publication. First, second, and third place winners as well as honorable mentions are noted in the biographies following the entries.

TABLE OF CONTENTS

SUSURROUS

Dreamscapes can be harsh
with the sound of angry door slams
or Father scolding us for laziness.
But my love's soft murmurs, and
the quilt's whisper as she turns,
are enough to bring me back.

The box fan is humming and my
tinnitus is ringing, but I can hear
the mourning doves outside,
and chorus frogs by the pond
announcing dawn. Crows bark
at each other across the bluescape.

Arising, I gather my clothes
from the floor beside the bed, move
slowly away so she is not disturbed.
Ripley watches with ears pricked
but is quiet. In the kitchen, I grab
a cup of yesterday's coffee, tiptoe
out the door, greet songbirds.

I am blasted by the brash demands
of bluejays at the feeder. A squirrel
approaches, stops short of a challenge.
My writing pad is bare. As the sun rises
above the treeline, shadows fall on
my paper, and move with the wind
like ghosts or omens.

Kelly Johnston

THE HARVEST

The flaming match on the horizon
settles behind thin clouds
burns down to a dark red glow.
The day heat escapes leaving
warm thick odors:
freshly cut prairie grass,
hog pens, coffee clouded
with Baileys, faint hints of perfume.

You sit outside awhile
running calloused fingers
over scarred hands.
Veins on your brown forearms
distended like seams of quartz.
You notice the wilting stems of the fallen
 crop, and remember how many times
you have harvested that field.

 Match light from igniting your pipe
casts shadows on the porch,
and you realize how dark it really is.

From her bedroom window,
the glow of your pipe looks
like the first star on the horizon.
She makes a wish, and you remember
her, and white sheets
and brown legs, and her hands
stained green from the harvest.

Kelly Johnston
This poem was previously published in 2017 by Blue Cedar Press in
the chapbook *Kalaska*.

RAGING AGAINST AGING

I will not fold up my wings like a dead quail
and fall into the depths of the prairie tallgrass.
I will pick up my shotgun, check for a hot load,
and keep hunting. I am hell-bent on raging
into many more sunsets and challenging many
more dawns from a cold duckblind alert
to movement and sound.

I will pick up my fishing pole, and wade
the muddy edge of my lake, interrupted
not by the phone or fax or deadline, only
by the splash of a bass attacking my jitterbug
or the honking of a flock of geese upset
by my presence and forced to fly on.
I will keep only a few fish to fry tonight.
Red-ear and bluegill I will toss ashore
for discovery by vultures or raccoons. I am
the master of this fishery.

I will keep walking behind my lawn mower,
miles and miles each growing season. I will
plant new petunias each spring, and thin out
my iris bulbs every fall. I will never hire
a gardener or neighbor kid to mow.
And every time I come home from the ranch,
I will hug LaDeena and lift her off the floor,
turn a circle like a dancer with her in my arms,
and kiss her gently for another 50 years. We
will charge the vast Uncertainty
hand-in-hand and side-by-side.
Bring it on!

Kelly Johnston is a life-long Kansan. He graduated from Wichita State University in 1977 with a major in creative writing and studied under A. G. Sobin, Anita Skeen and L.M. Grow. His poems have been published in the *California Quarterly* (Vol. 43, #3), *The Flint Hills Review* and the *I-70 Review*. His chapbooks *Kalaska* and *Tumbleweed* were both published by Blue Cedar Press. Kelly loves to spend time on his land in the Chautauqua Hills near Cross Timbers State Park where many of his poems have been inspired. Kelly's poems in this volume won first place for poetry in The Love Book Contest of Blue Cedar Press.

LATE

"This is going to hurt," my father says. "This is *really* going to hurt."

It will hurt, he's right about that though his mind's not right.

Before he came upstairs to bed, he'd been sitting in his chair babbling like a baby, his face bunched up in pain.

He doesn't know what's happening to him, and he hates it.

"This is going to hurt," he says again as I help him out of his pullover, his shirt, ease his jeans down over his skin and bones legs—no muscles left.

I pluck odd socks off his feet then pull back the covers for him. He slides in, pulls the sheet over his head, just the way I did as a boy.

I can't take his pain away. I hate to see him suffer.

"Have a good sleep, Dad. You'll feel better in the morning."

One late little lie.

Forgive me, father, for I have sinned.

I only did it, old curmudgeon, because I love you.

Brian Daldorph
(31 Oct 2013)

ON A GREY DAY

my golden girls,
my daughters,
come to me
at the kitchen table
with margarine tubs full
of *Crayolas*.

Color me
banana yellow,
cucumber green,
diamond blue!

Brian Daldorph
(9 March 1998)

LATE SLEEP

No time left for the things she loves,
only sleep.

No time left for family and friends,
only sleep.

No time left to go out into her garden—
her favorite place on earth—
only sleep.

No time left for salmon cooked by her daughter-in-law,
only sleep.

No time left for *Rummikub* and whist—
only sleep.

No time left for *Eggheads* or *Songs of Praise,*
for the Proms, for Mozart—
only sleep.

But she does open her eyes
to see the African marigolds in a vase:
"Lovely!"
then back to sleep.

(9 Aug 2015)

Brian Daldorph teaches at the University of Kansas, Lawrence, KS and at the DARE Center for people experiencing homelessness. His book about his jail teaching experience, *Words Is a Powerful Thing: Twenty Years of Teaching Poetry at Douglas County Jail* (U Kansas Press 2021), won the Kansas Book Award 2022. His poems in this book won second place in The Love Book Contest of Blue Cedar Press.

CARS DRIVING BY IN THE RAIN

Cars driving by in the rain
When I'm expecting you
Are louder than trains,
Their shrill whistles shushed
By each hopeful WHISH.

The clock ticks louder
Than the clackity-click
Of a boy dragging a stick
Down a picket fence
In the yellow-white glow
Of summer And I wonder

If maybe you fell asleep
Dreaming of me
And you were too pleased
To wake-up,
Or maybe you had a flat tire,
Or stopped to buy roses
From a roadside vendor.

I check my reflection
Twenty more times
To be sure it's perfect
And suddenly,
The train and the boy
And the roses and the clock
Scatter like cats
At the sound of your knock.

Cammie Funston

CRADLE OF THE MOON

The way I feel about you hasn't changed.
I still want to steal away
To some secret Shangri-La,
Lay on a blanket in the soft grass,
Stretch our arms into the azure sky,
And fold our fingers together in a dance
To Smokey Robinson and Frank Sinatra.

I long to linger for days
Talking and laughing,
And crying and cuddling,
Kissing lightly and softly,
Then falling silent in the night,
Like twin infants, spooning
In the cradle of the crescent moon.

Cammie Funston

GRAYSCALE

Not really jealousy
But a tiny heart flinch
A sticker in my sock
A brief hitch in my step
A hollow catch in my throat
A pot boiled over
A grain of salt in a paper cut
A dropped knit stitch
Her photos not mine
In sepia and grayscale
On the table
Beside his bed.

Cammie Funston, a native of Wichita, Kansas, holds a BS in Human Resources Management from Friends University and a BA in Communication Sciences and Disorders from Wichita State University. A retired educator, Cammie enjoys hand-building pottery, and is an advocate for persons with intellectual and developmental disabilities. These three poems won third place in The Love Book Contest of Blue Cedar Press.

HEALING HEARTS IN THE CARDIAC ICU: A LOVE STORY

Sheila Sharpe

"What you have is a heart problem," said the Urgent Care doctor, her stethoscope pulled back from my chest. "Can you feel it fluttering?"

"No, I'm only aware of shortness of breath and fatigue," I said.

"That's because your heart thinks you're running a race. You have Atrial-Fibrillation — an abnormally rapid heart rate. You need to go to the Emergency Room right now. Do not stop for lunch. Do not stop for anything."

Panic zinged through me. My problem sounded serious.

My husband, Michael, was with me. I'd felt too dizzy to drive. At the ER, we were quickly shuttled into a stall-sized space, the next narrow stall concealed behind a faded, pink curtain. Michael sat down in the one plastic chair, and I shed my clothes to put on one of those fiendish, open-backed hospital gowns that show off your butt. The blonde nurse stabbed me with an IV, while I lay propped up on the narrow bed, freezing in the refrigerated air. She, like most of the staff, wore a bright pink mask. A medical team of cheery masked faces seemed surreal in this overcrowded ER of bleeding, bandaged patients lined up on gurneys outside my cell. I should not be here, taking up a bed next to a seriously suffering patient who needed a heart transplant. I couldn't even feel my wacky heartbeat.

Shivering, helpless, and disoriented, I took comfort from Michael's solid presence and usual attire of a faded blue denim shirt, cargo shorts, and Birkenstocks. He'd worn a facsimile of this outfit for the 37 years he was a professor at UCSD. His thick mane of dark hair had now turned pure white and curled down his neck in the non-style of an old hippy academic. His steady support over the last four hours of intense worry and discomfort made me feel warmly towards him, a feeling I automatically kept in check. Neither of us were talented at sustaining emotional closeness.

Loud buzzing and dings started blasting from the monitors behind my bed. The help button didn't result in a nurse, so Michael waylaid one rushing by. She pushed and jiggled the equipment to no avail. "You get used to it." She laughed, saying she heard the dinging at home too." We could not laugh off the silly problem. We were going nuts.

Left to save our own sanity, Michael stood and studied the monitors. I turned on my side, craning my neck, while he gingerly pushed buttons and turned dials. "Try there!" I pointed to a red button lower down. He pressed it. Presto, the noise stopped. We grinned at each other and managed a truncated high five. The sense of a team gave me a lift, and I felt less alone.

The hours ticked by. The dinging resumed. I couldn't go home until the cardiac specialist saw me and my heart rate returned to normal. It's down somewhat, a nurse said brightly. Nerves frayed, my body aching, I had to get out of this claustrophobic coffin tonight. I'd spent weeks organizing a special tour of a friend's art exhibition to begin at the museum early the next morning.

My distress obvious, Michael moved closer to the bed and took my hand. I was surprised. He was not a hand-holder. Tears sprang to my eyes, and I squeezed his hand. The simple gesture felt significant. Spontaneous affection between us had sadly dwindled over the past decades of our marriage. Kisses and hugs were usually perfunctory. We'd both become wary of tender, romantic feelings, fearing that a sudden harsh disagreement might catch us off-guard and send us reeling back into our barren corners.

Ours was a marriage of opposites, though not in the sense of basic values, core beliefs, and certain shared interests like classical music. We were opposites in temperament, Michael being a brilliant, "rational" mathematician and me being a hot-blooded, "emotional" psychologist and artist. Also, we also did not share the same "language of love," as Gary Chapman calls it. Rather we had dissimilar expectations of how to love and be loved. Early on, I longed for romantic displays, like gazing at sunsets on the beach, arms linked, nuzzling, and sweet-talking each other. He thought sunsets garish and found the word "love" almost impossible to say.

A show-don't-tell Australian, he gave love through being helpful —as with my chronic computer problems and general technical ineptitude. But he was allergic to talk about feelings, my special talent. Of the many ways we failed each other, our fighting styles caused the most damage. I expressed my injuries with fierce attacks, akin to a dive-bombing Magpie, while Michael expressed his by retreating into a shell like a besieged tortoise. I found his silences unbearable, and my strident voice paralyzed him. Years of such interactions too often left both of us feeling lonely and unloved —the deepest of heart wounds.

Ironically, I was a successful couple therapist who wrote a book, *The Ways We Love,* that presents ways to heal damaged relationships. It's been tough, though not uncommon, to be a "love expert" who's failed to heal her own marriage. But Michael and I eventually wised up. Following my own advice for a change, we made a pact to stop the competitive fights about *who was right, who knew best,* and *who was to blame for whatever was wrong.* Sufficient battle scars and maturity were needed for this kind of agreement to work. But the downside of keeping a tighter control of anger and potential conflict was the possibility of suppressing warm, tender feelings as well. Consequently, with our sane and sensible cease fire came the sorrow of giving up my romantic ideal of emotional closeness.

At last, the cardiac kahuna showed up with his medical retinue. He wore a white coat, which was reassuring to an old-timer like me. A soother of frayed nerves, he tried to get me out of there that night. But it was not to be. My heart rate remained abnormally high despite many hours of IV treatments.

Moved to the cardiac ICU the next morning, I was gearing up to get my heart shocked back into a normal rhythm.

"This is not a big deal," said the pink-masked Fellow with cold blue eyes and a robotic voice. "A coating of lidocaine takes care of any discomfort." A medical team of six clustered around him. He planned to insert a tube down my throat to scope for blood clots, which might cause a fatal stroke. This was the first time I heard the word "fatal" or "stroke." I'd thought A-fib was common, medication fixed it, and people didn't end up in intensive care.

The thought of a tube shoved down my throat scared the bejesus out me, and I hated that annoying word "discomfort," which masked the probability of pain. Michael sat next to me and took my hand. "I'm right here." I lay rigid with fear as the cold-eyed Fellow started swabbing my throat with numbing lidocaine. The next moment, I was choking.

"I can't do this," I rasped. "I can't breathe."

"Lie still, your throat will be numb in a moment."

"Stop! Please! I can't breathe."

"You'll be fine as soon as the tube's inserted," said the robotic voice.

My throat clamped tighter. In agony, I struggled for air, flashing on the life-threatening asthma attacks I'd had as a child.

"Let's sit her up," said a sensible voice.

Sitting up, leaning forward, I fought to break through my blocked throat.

"Help me," I croaked.

"Just *relax*," said the kind-voiced nurse holding my other hand.

Had I any sense of humor or breath, I would have laughed.

"Get the breathing specialist," the Fellow ordered.

When the breathing specialist arrived, he tried to put an oxygen mask on my face. Frantic, I clawed at the suffocating contraption, hearing fragments of chatter among the group. A burst of laughter brought up the past image of an old TV episode of Mash, in which the surgical team chit-chatted and laughed while doing open-heart surgery. My team didn't seem to understand I was having a major panic attack and could die. I wanted to die; the pain was intolerable.

"Something is very wrong!" yelled my reserved husband. "Look at the color of her hands and feet."

The Fellow ordered Michael out of the room, and I passed out.

The next morning, I woke up in a bright room in the cardiac ICU. Alive, groggy, but breathing. I was ecstatic to see a blurry Michael sitting at the end of my bed. Thank God, I survived, and he was still with me. I could now clearly see his dear face drawn with tension, his curly white hair a tangled mess.

"Welcome back," said a cheerful nurse, raising the back of my bed. "We were worried." Later, she told me I had almost died.

When I was fully conscious, Michael described the Code Blue scene he'd witnessed after he left me with the alarmed medical team. "It was like one of those dramatic hospital scenes from the movies —the team racing down the corridor pushing the patient on a gurney. Your heart rate had gone sky high. I followed you to this room, where they put you on a ventilator for 16 hours."

"Yikes, glad I didn't know that." I'd heard about too many older people dying on ventilators. "All that drama must have been really scary for you."

"About as scary as it gets." He moved the stand with the IV lines and sat down next to me. We exchanged tremulous smiles and held hands, a feeling of closeness blossoming between us. I embraced the warm glow this time.

I spent the next five days in this room, trapped in a tangled nest of IV lines, and told not to move so my damaged heart could heal. I tried to cooperate but drew the line at wearing a diaper. This meant I had to let the nurses, including males, help me to the commode. Michael took over this task during the day. I wasn't thrilled with his seeing my saggy bottom or handing me toilet paper, but he was so kind and helpful, I quickly got over feeling exposed and humiliated. Michael stayed with me every day despite all the noxious nursing chores and odors and medical personnel buzzing around. When I caught him looking at me, I could see the concern and tenderness in his warm brown eyes. His steady gaze was more direct and connected, no longer blank or wary. This expression now struck me as far more loving than my adolescent fantasy of gazing at sunsets and cooing love-talk at each other.

A stream of nurses and doctors visited frequently to check my heart rate and other measures shown on an array of monitors next to my bed. Despite infusions of multiple medications, the numbers kept jumping around from a high of 180 to a low of 130 then back up the scale. I could hear their concerned voices whispering outside my door. "Her heart is failing," one doctor said. I cringed at this godawful news, but at least my marriage might be recovering.

I was worn down with the slow progress, sleeplessness, and body twitches and aches from inactivity. I'd be stuck in the ICU until my heart rate stayed reliably below 100.

The next shock to the heart lowered my heart rate below normal and lasted. Delirious, Michael and I spread our arms for the big hug we could not manage because of my IV lines. The next day, I was moved upstairs to a spacious, hotel-like room with a tiled bathroom I could now use all by myself. What heaven!

That evening we celebrated with the kitchen's best beef burgundy dinner set on a "romantic" white towel spread over a rolling cart. Smiling, we clinked water glasses, toasting each other's heroism and loyalty, and how the intolerable heartbreak of losing each other brought new life and love into our 57-year marriage.

Sheila Sharpe is an author, artist, and clinical psychologist residing in Del Mar, CA. She has an MFA in painting from UCSD and a PhD in psychology. Her publications include a professional book, *The Ways We Love,* and several articles and her stories have been featured in Fiction on the Web, Feminine Collective, and Memoir Mixtapes. This piece won first place for memoir in The Love Book Contest of Blue Cedar Press.

WAIT FOR ME

Marion Joseph Bollig

His new life began when the top of the dark box was opened and hands reached in to lift him into the light.

"Here Molly," said a man's voice. "It's your puppy."

A little girl squealed and clasped him to her chest, nuzzling his head. "He's so cute! Oh Daddy, I love him so much!"

"What will you call him?"

"I will call him Oliver," said Molly.

"You can call him Ollie for short," said Dad. "It'll be Molly and Ollie."

Ollie — a little white dog with curly hair, black button eyes and black nose — felt so much love. And so Ollie's new life began with hugs and kisses.

Ollie loved everyone in his new family — Dad, Mom, Big Sister and Little Brother — but especially Molly. At night Molly would put Ollie under the bed covers with her, and sometimes read him a story by flashlight. Molly would play in the yard with Ollie and toss him tennis balls and sticks. She and Ollie would play Tug-O-War with ropes and rags. They'd go on car rides together, and Molly would roll down the window so he could sniff new smells and feel the wind blow through his ears.

Molly would always share her French fries from the drive-through. She would whisper secrets in Ollie's ear, sing to him, talk with him about things on her mind. And Molly would hug Ollie when she was sad. She wouldn't have to say anything because Ollie understood.

What Ollie loved more than anything else was when Molly took him to a place at the edge of town, a huge field of grass that led to a hill. There was a winding trail, a shallow stream, and clumps of large, leafy trees here and there. The field was full of white and yellow flowers in the springtime. Molly would take off his leash and Ollie would race around in the field chasing rabbits, and birds, and grasshoppers. Molly would laugh because he never caught anything.

One day Mother said, "Molly dear, you don't look well. How do you feel?"

"I am tired all the time," Molly said. "I ache all over."

Ollie watched from the window as Mom and Dad took Molly to the doctor. They returned home later without Molly. They sat in the living room and cried together with Big Sister and Little Brother.

Over the next few months, the family would go to a big hospital to visit Molly. She would always smile when she saw them. They would put Ollie in her bed and she would fall asleep, smiling, with her arm around him.

One day while Ollie was snuggling against her, he felt Molly's heart stop.

Days, then weeks, then months, then years passed.

Ollie was an old dog. He lived with Dad and Mom only, because Big Sister and Little Brother had grown up and moved away.

When he slept he sometimes dreamt he was a young dog. He was in the great, grassy field chasing rabbits, and birds, and grasshoppers. But then, he saw her — far, far up the path.

It was Molly!

Ollie ran and barked, "Wait for me! Wait for me!"

Molly waved but kept walking up the path to the top of the hill. The faster he ran the farther she was. She would disappear over the hill.

Ollie would wake with a whimper. What did it mean?

One night he slept and dreamt again of the great, grassy field. He saw her again — Molly! Again, she was walking up the path to the top of the hill. Again, Ollie ran and barked, "Wait for me! Wait for me!"

This time Molly stopped. She turned. She began to run toward him!

Ollie ran furiously, barking and barking. Molly bent down and he leapt into her arms! She hugged him and kissed him, and Ollie made little cries.

"I missed you so much! I love you, Molly!" said Ollie.

"I missed you too, Ollie," said Molly. "I love you, too."

And together they walked the path up over the hill . . .

. . . and down into a beautiful, golden valley.

Marion Joseph Bollig is a graduate of the William Allen White School of Journalism and Mass Communications at the University of Kansas. After a short stint in radio, he worked for newspapers. He began writing short fiction and bad poetry in a desperate attempt to ward off terminal boredom. This piece won first place for short stories in The Love Book Contest of Blue Cedar Press.

HOW TO LOVE THE LOVE

I was born premature

                and learnt fast how to trick life.

Those who arrived on time, they became regular citizens.

And those who arrived late,

                kept forgetting their past.

I soaked myself in emptiness and slept with hunger,

took Pride as my midwife and Patience as my waitress.

Autumn begets autumn,

                spring always jumps forward,

and I slept on the earth of a rainswept summer.

And I took to Take—made everything mine.

But one thing I never learnt

                until I met you—

how to love the Love itself.

And I simply drowned in the amber of your light.

Biman Roy

GLOWING AND GROWING IN LOVE

That evening, your secret radiance
was almost suicidal.

The glow descended the staircase
in slow leopard paws,

opened the door to peek
at the crab apple tree playing

a shadow game with the rhododendrons.

You looked up at the sky
as if comparing notes—

two musicians at play,

in tandem, sounds embroidered. I was just a spectator,
floating like a balloon of pride and looking down.

I thought I possessed you
like seaweed wishes to possess the sea,

or like a roadside narcissus, lonely in its arrogance.

That night, I wished I could die

for you, when my heart refused to speak to me.

Biman Roy

LOVE WAS NEVER ENOUGH

Hums of a friendly laughter adorned the morning.

When I sat by your side,
                    you snuggled—

even in April, the cruelest month.

The beige of the bridge on the opposite side

                    was hurting my eyes.

I handed a river to you
and you returned with a century of toil

at the pulpit of surrender.

Love was never enough,

but patience sat at the door

like a bald, bare stone—

only and lonely.

Biman Roy's writings have been widely published, including his books *Navigating the Quartz Forest* and *Miss Manhattan*. His book of poems, *Miss Manhattan* has been translated into French, German, and Spanish. These poems are from the poet's recent manuscript, "Sorrow has a Weight of its Own," a deep reflection on the loss of his beloved wife to Covid.

SACHET

All of the dancing,

the curtsey and the bow,

the glance and the nod,

the genteel placing of hands,

the twirl and the frenzy,

the quick embrace,

the lingering sweet in stillness,

the careful ebb and flow,

lead to this precious

weighted moment,

within the fragrant linens.

Cammie Funston

WILDLIFE PRESERVATION

Hand in hand, paired by size, four little girls
wandered down the dusty path to the railroad tracks.
The boy tramped through the tall grass,
blazing his own trail to the abandoned line.

I watched them from the second story window,
mesmerized by the site of children and wildflowers
tumbled together in the Autumn breeze,
like denim and calico tossed in a dryer.

You pressed up behind me then.
I have lost track of you now.
Still, my Indian Summer days are
layered and laced with this memory.

Cammie Funston

WOODSMAN'S AMPHITHEATER

A renegade zephyr caressed your chest

and you quivered

before your axe split the ice air.

Wafts of honeysuckle

circled and softened

your face.

Stratus-laced indigo loomed,

like the garment of a sorceress

flung against the sky.

Her heart quickened,

watching your body arc

like an animated sculpture of Thor.

And you, wearing button-fly blues and bare skin,

stood sweating

in your frosty woodsman's amphitheater,

Performing your percussion solo

while the branches swayed and

the shadows cast ovations.

Cammie Funston, a native of Wichita, Kansas, holds a BS in Human Resources Management from Friends University and a BA in Communication Sciences and Disorders from Wichita State University. A retired educator, Cammie enjoys hand-building pottery, and is an advocate for persons with intellectual and developmental disabilities. These three poems won honorable mention in The Love Book Contest of Blue Cedar Press.

NIGHT TRAIN TO TRONDHEIM

Amy Stonestrom

My seat companion had a crew cut, a clean-shaven face made for glossy pages, and a cat in a carrier. He wore Norwegian military fatigues. I wore a long skirt and chunky-heeled canvas boots, a pair I bought in Sweden, where my friends and I had just finished a semester abroad. I didn't know his name and it didn't matter because in eight hours I would never see him again—but already I wanted to.

My friend Laurie twisted to make eye contact from the front of the crowded train car. She threw me a glare as she pointed to the hunched traveler seated next to her and nodded toward my attractive seat mate. I shrugged, smiled apologetically, and mouthed the words, Where's Kevin? Laurie shook her head and shrugged. She couldn't see him either. This was the pre-text era so we could only hope Kevin was in another compartment and wasn't standing alone on the platform while the train Laurie and I rode pulled away from the Oslo station. There was no way I was going to give up my seat to try to find him now.

Fatigues introduced me to his calico and offered me the window so I could see the "white night" as locals call it — the midnight sun. I have no idea how Norway's fields, streams, and red-roofed farm houses look beneath the long, low beams of light across the tall grass in white-night twilight. I barely peeked out the window.

Instead, I looked at the seat in front of me and met his eyes every so often, hoping my heart wouldn't land on my lap and flop onto the floor with each glance. I tilted my head toward him as he talked about his travels and his hopes for the future and asked me about mine.

It occurred to me at some point, from something vague he said about the calico, that the cat might belong to a girlfriend. It also occurred to me at some point that I had a boyfriend back in The

States. I never mentioned him.

Well past midnight, our car went dark. We kept our faces close and whispered our stories until our eyelids could no longer hold. I wanted to lay my head on his shoulder and fall asleep but I was too shy to make such an intimate move. When the sun and I both woke from our brief respite, I realized my head had found its place on his shoulder regardless and felt his head lean gently against mine. I could smell earth and soap on his neck.

How do you ask the sun to stop pouring out the hours? How do you ask today to delay its comeback till tomorrow?

I would still like to know.

Amy Stonestrom's essays have appeared in *Brevity, Superstition Review, Defunkt, Heavy Feather Review, Storm Cellar Quarterly* and elsewhere. She holds an MFA in creative nonfiction and has received awards from the 2022 Tucson Festival of Books, the National League of American Pen Women and *Street Light Magazine*.

WHAT I LOVE ABOUT YOU

for Jim

Elephants can hear
low frequency noises 4 km away

Bats use high-pitched echolocation
perfect for navigating darkness

Birds listen for distant storms
to begin migration

Baleen and Fin Whales employ sound waves
for long range reception

Tigers attract mates with infrasound
and crocodiles head-slap the water

I myself wear hearing aids
but often lose a connection

yet you, my love, without wings, fins, antennae
or manmade aids, can hear in a heartbeat

what I need, even when I am silent,
or thousands of miles away.

Donna Langevin

IF I WERE A HOUSE

for André

I'd be my son's cottage on Georgian Bay.

I would stand tall and stark
in my painted white coat
shadowed by creamy birches
and the creaking masts of poplars
with wind-frayed leafy sails.

Shoulder to shoulder with mammoth
Precambrian boulders, I'd hear
the waves carving my shoreline
and eating away the archipelago
made by a mythical giant
who dropped a mountain that shattered.

In summer, I'd welcome hummers
to the red plastic petunias my son hung
from my balcony and I'd watch
a hawk sizing up jays gorging
on suet and corn while a Grey Fox waits
to pounce on a chipmunk stealing
the spilled kernels.

When my son drives up from his city life
to replenish his feeders
and spend a weekend with me,
I'd listen for the crunch of his footsteps
on the gneiss-pebbled path.
My blue door would throw itself open,
all my windows light up.

Donna Langevin

CIRCLE

At eighteen months, my grandson
can't tell time but at 5 o'clock sharp
he listens for the turn of the front door key
and his father's soft-soled footsteps.

Abandoning his matchbox cars,
favourite toy piano
and Big Bird on Sesame Street,
he runs down the hall
like a bear cub to honey.

My son, who grew up without a father,
scoops up his toddler and laughs:
How's my Prince Pepito?
As he imitates a trumpet's bright tones
playing a royal fanfare, I recall
forty years ago, when I came back from teaching
my son toddled into the daycare room
and stretched out his arms.

His silky cheek pressed against
my powdered one,
sticky hands in my hair
milky breath mingling with mine,
I still see the purple circle
my lipstick left on his forehead
as I called him "my little King."

Donna Langevin's latest poetry collections are *Brimming* published by Piquant Press, 2019 and *Timed Radiance*, Aeolus House 2022. She won first place in *The Banister* anthology competition 2019 and also in the Ontario Poetry Society Pandemic poem contest 2020. *A Story for Sadie* was published by Piquant Press in 2023. Her poems won honorable mention in The Love Book Contest of Blue Cedar Press.

LATIN LOVERS

Scott Hurd

Italian is the language of lovers. Think opera and poets, Puccini and Petrarch. Or, think Kevin Kline purring "mozzarella" and "provolone" to a comically rapturous Jamie Lee Curtis in *A Fish Called Wanda*. My wife and I, however, stumbled onto another love language altogether. A language which is, in fact, officially considered dead: Latin. More logical than lyrical, Latin is better suited to law than love. Or so I've heard. Because I don't speak Latin, and neither does Diane. But as our love language, the tiny snippet we know is working well for us so far.

It was language that first brought us together, or at least placed us in the same room. It wasn't Latin but one of its Romance children, French. Specifically, freshman year French. Both of us had taken French in high school, so our taking this entry-level class was a shameless bid for an easy "A." She got her "A." I ended up with a "B," entirely from lack of effort. Yet my teenage laziness did place me in near proximity to the woman who, thirty-two years later, would become my life partner. Surely that justifies my lack of scholarly effort. Even if just a little bit.

I wish we could report that, while conjugating *aimer*, our eyes met and sparks flew, sowing seeds of an unrequited love that left us pining for each other over three decades. But no. We ascertained that we were in class together much later, after searching for common denominators of four parallel years at a smallish university. As it was, we sat on opposite sides of the classroom and didn't recognize the other's presence. She insists that my attention was focused on the cute swimmer seated to my right, which isn't entirely untrue.

After that, our paths didn't cross again in college. We did share a handful of mutual friends, however, meaning that there was only one degree of separation between us on several fronts. In fact, I hung out with some of her sorority sisters, one of whom helped me satisfy a traditional graduation requirement: a gazebo kiss on the little island halfway across the campus lake. Yet as students Diane and I never met in person, let alone our lips.

US military intervention was required for our first conversation, seventeen years after we'd received our diplomas. A high school buddy of mine, an officer in the Army Reserve, was soon to be deployed to Kosovo. Through a combination of coincidence, good luck, and perhaps a hint of providence, he had married one of Diane's best college friends. She was throwing him a big farewell party, and Diane and I were both invited. When I arrived, her magnificent blond hair, full and flowing and naturally curling, immediately caught my eye. She was with another guy; I was with my first wife.

I recognized her as a classmate and introduced myself. We chatted, exchanged pleasantries, and nothing more. And that was it for a few years. Then, in Facebook's infancy, her face popped up as a friend suggestion. Since we had several shared connections, I sent a request. Not because I had inappropriate intentions, but because I had a hidden agenda. I had a book coming out, and collecting social media contacts was a shameless marketing ploy. But she wasn't aware of that when she clicked "accept." And neither of us had a clue of what that key press would lead to.

It turned out that Diane is a writer too, and over the next few years we swapped friendly messages about our shared craft. So it was entirely understandable that, days before our 25th class reunion, she asked if I was coming. We hadn't seen each other since our friends' party, and she was hoping to catch up face-to-face. But I was not going. My then-wife and I had just separated, a progressive stage in a protracted, painful, public, and initially unwanted divorce. It was the lowest point in my life. Politely referring to this as a "family crisis," I asked for Diane's prayers.

She wrote back, expressing concern and support. I replied; she answered. We quickly established that we shared more than an alma mater and a love of writing. We also bore deep heartbreak scars from discarding and distress, ghosting and grief. Both of us, advancing on fifty, contemplated our diminishing prospects for a coupled future. We listened. We commiserated. We encouraged. Sharing our pain made bearing it bearable. And our blossoming friendship assured us that we were more lovable than we had thought.

After a short time of this, she ended an email in a way I did not expect: "Peace, Diane." I was floored. "Peace" is how I typically closed my messages. Just not to her, yet. I feared how she might react. Would she think it weird? Too groovy? Too pious, or even sanctimonious? Until then, I'd concluded my emails to her with only my name, stumped for what else to say. It was too early for "love" or even "fondly." "Best wishes" sounded too formal, and "sincerely" is strictly for business, at least in my book. But Diane had beat me to the punch with "peace." With one little word I knew I'd found a kindred spirit.

She'd later admit that she'd never before ended an email that way and had no idea why she did it. Maybe it was an unconscious manifestation of long yoga practice or a distant echo of hippyish Deadhead days. Perhaps an unseen hand had guided her. My doing so was inspired by Francis of Assisi, the thirteenth century Italian saint known for his simplicity, care for creation, and commitment to nonviolence. Instead of greeting others with "hello," Francis recommended *pace e bene* — Italian for "peace and good." I liked that. I thought that by wishing each other peace, maybe there'd be more to go around, kind of like a self-fulfilling prophecy.

Francis' devotees would Latinize *pace e bene* into *pax et bonum*. Yet when I introduced that phrase to Diane, I quoted it as *pax et bene*: two thirds Latin, one third Italian. Spanish speakers learning English claim to speak "Spanglish," but what was my mashup? Latalian? Pidgin Latin? Confusing things even further, I asserted that *bene* is Latin for "blessing," and we agreed that "peace and blessing" was a lovely sentiment for friends to share. However, soon thereafter I was reminded that *bene* is Italian for "good" and that *pax et bonum* was the correct Latin form. I had been wrong yet again.

But Diane didn't care. She spliced my mumbo jumbo together into "Pax et Bonum et Bene." It stuck. "Peace and Good and Good." Or "Peace and Good and Blessing." Whichever. We'd conflated two languages, but created something uniquely ours. "Pax et Bonum et Bene" now concluded all our messages. But while we thought it charming, we agreed that it was a bit long. Soon it was shortened to P+B+B, and then simply PBB. Our phrase became an equation and then an abbreviation, decipherable only by us.

By this time, Christmas was approaching. In a gambit to nudge our relationship beyond the friend zone, I sent her a decorative

Italian ceramic tile proclaiming "Pax et Bonum," because only the correct Latin was available. As Diane shared later, it was the best gift she's ever received. Two months later, she confessed to having a crush on me. We soon had our first date. Our mutual friends, at whose party we'd first met, showed up, because of course there's nothing better than chaperones at midlife. Fifteen months later we were engaged. We'd kiss on that gazebo. And we got married in our college chapel.

"I speak Latin to God, Italian to women, French to men, and German to my horse," boasted Holy Roman Emperor Charles V. Well, bully for him. My French is lousy, my German is nonexistent, and I don't know where Latin ends and Italian starts. But none of that really matters. Because Diane's Italian tile with its Latin text now rests by our front door. No longer do we conclude our emails with "PBB;" it's how we wish each other goodnight. While our love language may be officially dead, our love is very much alive. Taking a cue from Saint Francis himself, I'm happy to say: It's peaceful. It's good. And it's blessed.

Scott Hurd is the award-winning author of five books published in four languages, including *Forgiveness: A Catholic Approach*. Recent essays are featured in *The Examined Life, Streetlight Magazine, The Smart Set, Allium, Cleaver, KAIROS, Salvation South, Ohio History, Medicine and Meaning, Brevity* (blog) and *Pembroke Magazine*. This piece won third place for memoir in The Love Book Contest of Blue Cedar Press. A version of this essay was published in *University of Richmond Magazine* in May 2024.

DANCING IN THE DARK

Barbara Bourne

I thought I would tell you a love story, but then I remembered — it might be that only Cecil was in love and, even then, he may have been more in love with the concept of Lizzie than with Lizzie herself.

As for Lizzie, she was an independent woman, born with her brain in perpetual motion, which she sometimes confused with emotion, which, in turn, she sometimes confused with love. And, perhaps, that's what had happened in her brain — and her heart — the day she met Cecil.

But I could be wrong. Maybe this was true love for both of them.

This particular story — I'll let you decide for yourself whether it is a love story or not — is about their first anniversary, which Lizzie knew was celebrated with gifts of "paper." But, while Lizzie was purchasing a most-charming book of sonnets — a sweet little leather bound edition of poetry on *paper* — Cecil was out hunting for something made of *cotton* — the traditional gift of second anniversaries. After weeks on the hunt, he'd finally found the perfect thing in a dusty antique shop deep in the heart of Boston's Back Bay: a set of hand-embroidered tea towels, which, he was especially pleased to note, were stitched with deep red threads, perfectly matching the rose-painted teacups they'd bought together in that very same shop the previous summer.

Cecil was nothing if not romantic.

You might be asking: Why the confusion over first or second; paper or cotton? November 8, 2015, was indeed their first anniversary. Lizzie's gift of paper was perfectly appropriate, more so than Cecil's you would say if unaware that Lizzie and Cecil had met two years earlier on November 8, 2013, exactly one year before their wedding.

So, Cecil was celebrating two wonderful years with the perfect woman although, he admitted, she often left her dishes in the sink and squeezed toothpaste from the middle. Still, he remained confident they would eventually evolve as life-companions, if only she'd stop kicking off her shoes and leaving them wherever they landed. And, of course, the socks, which usually ended up nowhere near the shoes.

Lizzie, too, was generally happy with their marriage and was proud they'd made it through the first twelve months. Like any thirty-somethings who'd lived independent lives prior to moving in together, they were learning to accommodate one another's quirks and habits.

Their morning routine said it all. Lizzie arose early, showered quickly, and made herself a large mug of black coffee before taking Big Sam out for his morning constitutional. Oh, did I forget to mention that Lizzie's large lovable dog of undetermined lineage accompanied her into the marriage? And, much to Cecil's chagrin, liked to sleep next to Lizzie on the bed?

Cecil, on the other hand, slept in most mornings, rarely starting his day before 9:00, and usually with a long, leisurely bath. Once downstairs, he'd unfold the morning paper with a flourish, breakfast on two slices of lightly toasted white bread, and enjoy a cup of Earl Grey with just a splash of milk. He'd then offer a larger splash to Athena, his elderly Siamese cat, before washing up his dishes — along with the cup Lizzie invariably left in the sink — and head upstairs to work on his novel.

Now, before we get into this particular love-story-of-sorts, I should tell you about the house Cecil inherited from his uncle, who'd died — quite conveniently — one month before the wedding. Not only did his passing save the bridal couple the cost of one chicken-beef-or-vegetarian-option dinner at the reception, it allowed them to slide into homeownership long before they ever could have afforded it on the combined incomes of a fledgling graphic designer and an aspiring-novelist-by-day/SAT tutor-by-evening-and-weekends.

Uncle Bertrand's house was an old Victorian located near Cummings Park, an area once home to bankers, doctors, lawyers, and those who needed no employment at all to afford life's luxuries. But the neighborhood had declined and, by the time Cecil inherited it, the houses nearest the park were in need of renovation and the ones closer to Maple Street were ready for the bulldozer. Uncle Bertrand's house sat somewhere in the middle.

"Perfect," said Cecil when they pulled into the driveway.

"We'll see," replied Lizzie as she stumbled over vines tangled across rickety porch steps.

"We'll move in right after the honeymoon," Cecil declared with the excitement of a child discovering Disneyland.

"Only if we get Uncle Bertrand's things out first and update the plumbing," said Lizzie, who admitted that the house had potential.

"We can't let go of this furniture, Elizabeth. We'll refinish! Reupholster! They don't make furniture the way they used to."

Lizzie agreed but said Uncle Bertrand's bed had to go and demanded they hire a professional cleaning service and put an exterminator on retainer.

"Good idea," said Cecil, and closed the deal by suggesting they employ a chimney sweep as well. Lizzie rolled her eyes and started humming "Chim-Chim-Cheree" before giving him a kiss.

"I love you, Elizabeth," Cecil said, content with the outcome of their negotiation. "I love you too, Cecil," she replied with a tinge of trepidation.

So, there they all were on November 7, the eve of whichever anniversary you want to call it — Cecil, Lizzie, Big Sam, and Athena — existing relatively peaceably together in an old, somewhat-livable Victorian with worn furniture, updated plumbing, no bugs, and a cozy fire in the working fireplace.

As predicted, a big nor'easter was barreling up the New England coast. The lights had flickered several times and, based on previous experience during snowstorms, thunderstorms, and a few gentle rains, Cecil and Lizzie both knew it wouldn't be long before they'd lose their electricity.

"I'm going to get ready for bed before the lights go out," Lizzie told Cecil and dashed upstairs to wrap the little book of sonnets.

"I'm going to make a cup of tea," Cecil told Lizzie and headed towards the kitchen to take a final look at the tea towels before wrapping them.

Ten minutes later, Lizzie was heading for Cecil's study, planning to slip her present onto his desk. She smiled, picturing his surprise at her uncharacteristic attempts at romance. Knowing how Cecil loved all-things-fancy, she'd wrapped the book in elegantly embossed paper and tucked a flowery card under a carefully tied silk ribbon.

Down in the kitchen, Cecil was placing six freshly-laundered and perfectly-pressed cotton tea towels into a box. Knowing how Elizabeth loved anything artsy, he wrapped the box with the hand-printed, overpriced paper he'd bought at her favorite boutique and tied it with the red twine the hipster clerk had said would look "just awesome" with the paper.

Then, remembering that the anniversary poem he'd written for her was tucked away in his desk drawer, he hid the present in the butler's pantry, grabbed his tea, and headed upstairs.

At this point, you might be thinking, How Romantic. Or maybe you're predicting this marriage is doomed. I'll just say that love is complicated. This is merely a snapshot of one evening in the life of two people who can't know the future but, for reasons they sometimes forget and — thankfully — sometimes remember, are sticking together from one day to the next.

"Drat!" Lizzie mumbled under her breath, unable to push open the door to Cecil's study. She'd hoped to slip in and out quickly before he came up to bed but the door wouldn't budge.

"Double drat," she said, hearing Cecil's teacup rattle in its saucer as he walked down the hall. Lizzie quickly shoved his present into her sweater pocket, irritated that she was crushing the bow she'd worked so hard to tie.

"Darn it, Cecil," she turned, exasperated. "The door is totally stuck."

"Step aside, Elizabeth. I'll take care of it." Cecil replied without questioning why she wanted to get into his study. He handed her his teacup, slipped out of his leather slippers, and placed them neatly against the baseboard molding. Then, spreading bare feet wide, he gritted his teeth, furrowed his brow, and shouldered his full bantamweight into the door. It shuddered once and emitted a woeful squeak, but didn't move. A second attempt yielded nothing more than a second squeak.

"Three's a charm?" asked Lizzie, hoping he'd just open the door and retreat back downstairs.

One more shoulder-shove, one more squeak, one more shake of the head.

"It's the storm," Cecil man-splained as he rubbed his shoulder and winced slightly. "You see, Elizabeth, the wood is swollen from age and damp weather. All the layers of paint on the door and doorjamb are rubbing together, thus causing the squeaks."

Pleased with his explanation, Cecil stepped back into his slippers, retrieved his delicate cup and saucer from Lizzie's hand, and was too immersed in self-satisfaction to notice her exasperated eye roll.

"Pretty windy out there," he said as the howling storm increased in pitch and intensity.

"Oh my God, Cecil!" She turned back to face him. "That's not wind! That's the soundtrack to our lives and I'm playing the lead in your cheesy movie. I've had it!"

Lizzie waved her hands in no particular direction as branches scraped windows and rain pounded the roof.

"And, do you hear that?" She started moving her finger in time to a rhythmic creak-and-bang, creak-and-bang. "I told you last summer we had loose shutters. Now one's broken free and will be slamming against our bedroom window all night."

Lizzie threw up her hands in frustration and headed towards the staircase. "I'm getting a screwdriver."

Cecil gasped. "You're not planning to fix the shutter in this hurricane, Elizabeth?"

Lizzie turned back and spit out, "No, Cecil. I am not that crazy. I'm going to unscrew the hinges on this darn door and get it open."

And for once, Cecil did see her eye roll…just moments before the lights went out for good.

"Where are you, Elizabeth? I can't see." Cecil's voice bordered on whining. "I have a touch of night blindness, you know."

"Yes, Cecil. I know. How about you stay right here, and I'll grab a flashlight while I'm getting the screwdriver."

Lizzie felt her way along the hall to the stairs, slid her hand down the banister for guidance and slowly descended in the dark. She counted each step. One, two, three…and knew to turn left when she reached seven. Then eight, nine, ten, and, oh… a deliciously wicked thought. The next step — third from the bottom — was the one that groaned loudly if you stepped on it just slightly to the left of center. Unable to resist, she aimed for the sweet spot…and there it was. C-c-r-r-e-e-a-k!

She immediately heard a stifled yelp from above, the clink of bone china shattering on hardwood floors, and a string of modest curses.

"You okay up there, Cecil?" she asked aloud as she silently chastised the devil perched on her shoulder.

"Dropped my teacup. I'm fine," replied a quavering voice. "We'll need a dustpan."

And here, my friends, comes the pivot point in our story, the place where Lizzie finds herself teetering between indulgence and exasperation, between love and the opposite of love, which we all know is not hatred, it is how-did-I-get-myself-into-this-relationship or God-give-me-strength or maybe even I'm-so-out-of-here.

But this is also the point where a little magic touched Lizzie's heart and tipped the scales.

Lizzie had made it downstairs. The living room — "we call it the parlor, Elizabeth," Cecil's voice corrected in her head — was awash in dim gray-yellow light. The pines outside danced a frenzied tarantella in the wind. The big oak's swirling branches stretched wide, its clinging leaves twisting wildly with each new gust. Inside, tangled shadows shifted, turned, and multiplied several times over as they bounced off the warped glass of several elaborately-framed mirrors.

Mesmerized, Lizzie stared at the complicated choreography of the leaf shadows dancing across the room. Like hundreds of Freds and Gingers, they twirled elegantly across the carpet then, as the wind's strength and direction shifted, as frail light reflected and refracted, pirouetted across windowpanes and mirrors, the Fred-leaves — or were they Gene Kelly's she wondered — danced up the damask-covered walls, across the high ceiling, and back into their Ginger's leafy arms.

Lizzie sat down on the faded settee and remembered that it was indeed Fred who'd danced up the walls, across the ceiling, and into the arms of, not Ginger, but Jane Powell. Gene Kelly was *Singin' in the Rain*, she recalled, the first movie she'd ever watched with Cecil.

And here it was. The magic moment when the dancing leaves, the music now running through her head, the gilded mirrors and worn settee all reminded her of why she'd fallen for Cecil in the first place.

Unlike the boys she'd dated in college with their beer parties and football games, Cecil had suggested they attend a classic movie festival for their first date. After two showings, they went to his favorite speakeasy-type bar, where he bought them vodka gimlets and then, quite literally, swept her off her feet with jitterbugs and Lindy Hops, the East Coast Swing and the Carolina Shag.

Within days, he was introducing her to his magical world of romance and elegance. "Romance and elegance" on an aspiring writer's budget meant surviving for weeks on ramen in order to have a single evening of champaign, foie gras, and caviar; it meant purchasing two — now one, Lizzie reminded herself — almost-matching teacup and saucer sets in a Back Bay antique shop.

And the books. Cecil had given books new meaning, new life. Lizzie had always loved to read, but Cecil taught her that a good book is more than plot and characters. Books for Cecil were a sensory adventure and now, she too visited old bookstores in order to run her fingers across cracked bindings worn thin with age, inhale the heady aroma of leather and musty paper, feel the heft of a lengthy novel, or thrill over the fragility of a tiny book of poems.

Lizzie smiled, thinking how much Cecil would love the sonnets she'd bought and wrapped so lovingly. She patted the package in her pocket and sighed. Her life was richer now. It was sensuous in ways she never could have imagined before she got swept up in Cecil's world. She thought about love and life and the little things that make a relationship work. Her heart swelled.

"It's still really dark up here, Elizabeth," Cecil's tinny voice broke through her reverie.

Lizzie stifled the snarky response that popped into her head. "Be right there, Ceese," she called up to him.

"I keep telling you, Elizabeth. It's Cecil," he corrected.

Lizzie rolled her eyes once more, just as the lights came back on. She grabbed a screwdriver from her toolbox under the sink and quickly headed back up the stairs, careful this time to avoid the spot slightly left of center on step number three.

Barbara Bourne is a retired educator currently living in North Carolina. She has written and edited several education-related books and only recently discovered the joys of writing fiction. She is a member of the Burlington Writers Club in Alamance County, NC. This story won second place for short stories in The Love Book Contest of Blue Cedar Press.

43

A HEART

Lyrics from "Anyone Who Had a Heart" swirl

through my head this cloudy, gray morn.

Memories, stirred to scorn our lives.

Separate, split, as though never one at all,

but in a dream once…now gone.

Anyone who had a heart could not be content with this rent,

this tear, this break, this ache.

What was it you said?

"No one can ever take you away from me."

But you must not have thought of *you*. Nor did I.

Trust, at a level so deep.

Now the love so strong haunts and taunts us—still a force,

alive in memories, in a child. Remember her?

You have thrust her away as well,

and made your life your way.

Do you feel hurt or dull aches?

A regret? A pull at your heart?

I am sad for us, for the love cast out. I could shout,

or scream, or shriek—a model for Munch.

Yesterday, our anniversary, I thought of us,

our wedding, our life, our dream.

The hurt comes when I dwell on it,

long dead, long gone. Stilled.

A phantom only living in the chambers of

anyone who has a heart.

Barbara Waterman-Peters' poems have been published in *150kansaspoems*, *The Writers Place Yearbook 2022*, *Kansas Speaks Out*, *Ichabods Speak Out*, and *The Write Bridge*. She writes about art and artists for *TOPEKA Magazine* and *the Kansas Reflector*, and writes and/or illustrates children's books, including *The Fish's Wishes*, *Bird*, *Ting & the Caterbury Tales* (with author Glendyn Buckley), and *A Packrat Named Orange* (with author Cathy Callen). Her creative non-fiction piece, "Winter Guests," was nominated for a Pushcart Prize and her art is on the cover of multiple publications.

DYKE MARCH, 2021

Leslie Cagan

On Saturday, June 26, I went to the 29th Annual NYC Dyke March. Well, I didn't actually go to the whole march. It was hot and humid and I didn't feel like I'd be able to do the full 2+ miles, so I headed to Washington Square Park where it would end, planning to join for the last few blocks

I got there earlier than I thought I would, and immediately found a parking spot. (Sometimes it's the small things that bring me great pleasure.) I was on Fifth Avenue a few blocks north of the park, perfect spot. Figured I could take a little nap in the car, but for some reason wasn't able to fall asleep. Instead I watched as people and traffic went by, New York City having turned a corner on the COVID crisis. The pandemic was far from over but here in the city things were changing for the better.

It turned out I was parked at a church and there was a social event on the lawn in the front courtyard. People gathered, all looking happy to see one another. Hugs were shared, lots of chatter, some people at tables and others standing around as the food was being prepared. The church had a banner out front that said they Celebrate LGBTQI+ Pride, and another one saying Refugees and Immigrants Are Welcome. Above the main entrance to the church hung a big Black Lives Matter sign. It all looked good.

Fully aware that I knew nothing about these people or the dynamics between them, I noticed that of the forty or so people there, I saw only five or six people of color. But what really stood out was that all of these folks (except the one man of color who was clearly working at the gathering) were sitting at a table together and, while some of the white people came over and chatted for a bit, none of them sat down. The scene provoked me to wonder what a true racial reckoning means in our daily lives. To be clear, I had no basis to assume bad intentions or behavior. But this small snapshot reminded me how complex our interactions with one another really are.

I looked the other way and realized I was right across the street from one of the NYU dorms. A memory from 1967/68 came rushing to the surface. I was a student at NYU and lived at home, but one of my closest friends was living in the dorm. During our activism against the U.S. war in Vietnam we had connected, strongly connected. One evening we were in her room when I found the courage to tell her I was attracted to her. All these years later I don't recall the exact words, but I know I was clear that I wanted to sleep with her. (When I was seventeen I had my first sexual relationship with a woman so I fully understood what my feelings were at this moment.) She seemed nervous, maybe scared, maybe both, and gently said no. That was okay. I wanted something else, but I was fine and knew that our friendship was solid. Our connection was real and we would stay in one another's lives as friends.

A year or two later I returned to NYC after a trip away and learned that my friend was hospitalized because of an emotional breakdown. I went to see her but when I told the front desk who I was there to visit they said that would not be possible. I never learned the details, but someone had decided that it would not be good for her to see me. I felt awful and confused: why could I not see my friend? I never did find out who made that decision or why, and while she and I saw each other from time to time over the next few years, we didn't talk about it. To this day I can't help but wonder if in some way it was connected to what had happened that night in her dorm.

There I was, waiting for the Dyke March and remembering how long being a lesbian was part of my self-definition. It seemed like it was taking forever for the march to arrive, so I got out of the car and walked up and down Fifth Ave. for a bit. I noticed a photographer also waiting for the march and it occurred to me that I should suggest that she take a photo of me with a caption that could say, "Old Dyke Waiting for Dyke March." But by the time I decided to actually approach her with this idea, she had disappeared. I still think it would have been cute.

Finally, the march was approaching. As is pretty much always the case with any group marching in the streets of NYC, there were police officers in the front. Not a heavy presence and it didn't feel tense or troubling, just another piece of the picture. (Let me be crystal clear: I am deeply critical of the ways the NY Police Department interacts with public protests and other events, as well as other terrible policing practices.)

Coming up next was the Dykes on Bikes contingent — in the lead as they have always been. The bikes were loud and the exhaust fumes not very pleasant, but it was thrilling to see them! So out there, so proud, so excited, and simply so beautiful. I waved to an old friend and when they stopped to wait for the rest of the march to catch up, she jumped off her bike and came over to give and get a big hug. I could feel the energy of the Dykes on Bikes, and the hug, in this coming-out-of-COVID period, was wonderful.

And then the waves of people marching behind the great big Dyke March banner. I had already run into and had a conversation with some old friends who were ahead of the march by a few blocks. They had said it looked like a pretty small turn out. But as the march went by I started to wonder if they had seen what I was seeing. It was not the biggest march ever, but it certainly was not small! Went on for blocks and blocks and blocks.

Maybe half-way or two-thirds of the way into the march came the drummers, lots of drummers (at least thirty-five to forty people). Lots of bold, strong energy coming right at me, and it felt contagious, in a good way!

As the march kept coming, I found myself getting happier and happier. Right before my eyes, literally thousands of overwhelmingly young people in the Dyke March…and it brought great joy to this aging dyke. I admit that my instinct is to call them "women," but I am using "people" because I have no idea how all of those folks identify, and identity has gotten even more complex and textured than it always has been. I'm sure lots of them are dykes or lesbians, consciously choosing one or both of those words. But the main thing is that all of them had chosen to participate in the Dyke March with tons of dyke-loving energy and pride and boldness right out front. In this time when I, and others, are wondering with some trepidation about something we call "disappearing lesbians,"   it was thrilling to see so many passionate, delighted revelers on Fifth Ave. behind the Dyke March flag.

And it was wonderful to see the breadth of how people were expressing themselves. The theme of this year's march was "Black Dyke Power," and the diversity in race as well as in style. and attitude, and way of presenting to the world – it all made me feel grateful and proud. Holding that diversity gave a palpable sense of community. I have no idea how deeply, or if at all, those marchers were experiencing that space as community, but for these few hours there was no ignoring the vividly evident love, mutual appreciation, and solidarity.

Over the years I've missed a lot of the Dyke Marches, but I know the organizers and the participants have always been attentive to the politics of race and sexual/gender identity, and how from the beginning it was always a space where every dyke-identified person was welcomed and celebrated. As I watched and then jumped into the march, I also remembered, and knew from my own experience over many decades, that dykes have been part of every struggle for justice throughout history. I found pride welling up in me as I marched with old friends and thousands of young people knowing that this community will continue to keep fighting to help make sure everyone is free.

The great joy I felt from all of this was only strengthened by running into a number of old friends, connecting as we quickly tried to catch up, and giving and receiving lots of hugs. OMG, the hugs are a lifeline. It's partly that we have been living through a global pandemic which has already taken close to 4 million lives, many of which directly resulted from the criminal negligence of the Trumps and Bolsonaros and Modis of the world. And it's partly that we are still reeling from and still dealing with the Trump years as well as the aftermath and ongoing horror he unleashed in this country.

As all of this was rumbling through my body, I was also remembering what this date, this event, means for my own life. Twenty-four years ago, poet/scholar/organizer Melanie Kaye/ Kantrowitz and I, having earlier had just one lunch date, had made plans for our second date at the Dyke March. I don't recall why, but we had decided not to march together but instead to hook up in Washington Square Park at the end. I marched with friends and pretty much the whole way talked about how I was about to meet up with Melanie and how excited I was. She marched with her friends.

Sure enough, we found one another and said goodbye to our friends. I recall words of encouragement from mine, as they could already see something was going to happen.

Melanie and I spent another hour or more sitting in a quieter section of the park talking. We got hungry, found a Thai restaurant, and as we ate we kept talking. Then we walked around the Village for some time, talking. And finally, it was time to go home. We danced around it for a moment, and I don't recall who said it first, but we both knew we were going home together. She was staying with some friends in their small apartment. While they were great people, we knew that would not work. I was staying for a stretch with an old friend who luckily was out of town for the weekend so I had the apartment to myself…that's where we went.

It should come as no surprise that once there we talked and talked and talked. We were in the living room and at one point I was on the floor rolling a joint and she got off the couch, sat next to me, leaned over, and kissed me. In a split second we were kissing each other, and not much longer after that we went to the bedroom.

And that's how the Dyke March became our anniversary. We went to many of them together over the years, until going to anything became too hard for Melanie to manage. On July 10, it will be 3 years since she died. I get chills just writing that short sentence. While the pain and deep sadness has subsided over these three years, I still miss her very much.

Being at this year's Dyke March was also about something additional for me. Yes, I missed Melanie through it all, but the strongest emotion of the evening was the thrill of seeing all of those young people with all of their passion and energy carrying forward the power and joy the Dyke March has always embodied for so many.

Leslie Cagan is a long-time organizer for peace and justice. This piece won second place for memoir in The Love Book Contest of Blue Cedar Press.

POWDER RIVER

--for Brock

on our way back from sumpter
we stop to walk along powder river—

an obsidian dipper bobs
on boulders in the navy glisten—

a noiseless crested kingfisher cruises
low over the rippling—

I crunch consciously through snow—
aware of every step—

we wind our way through
ponderosa pines—

I stop to smell one because
they are fragrant vanilla

in the sun, but this one
stands in shadows—

the skeletons of last year's pinedrops:
little black balls on long tall stems—

my grief is a lump
in my throat—

slick and clear, like ice—
it chokes me—

my grief is a cold black river
rippling through me

with brittle icy edges—
I feel it moving through me—

and then I see you ahead
walking in the puffy pumpkin coat

and my grief begins to melt—
you wear mismatched black

gloves and a red hat with ear flaps—
you test the ground to make sure

it is safe for me to walk
by running your boots over the uneven

ice—you turn and smile at me—
I creep unsteadily along—

you give me the courage
I need to go on.

Shanan Ballam

THE GARDEN

How could I live without you, this garden,
purple-black pansies in rocks, glint
of brilliant buds, scarlet penstemon.
In blue dusk, sphinx moths buzz in catmint.

The moment they lift. The moment after.
For this, I live: radishes underground blush
their bulbed heads, little crimson lanterns,
a spicy light I will lay on my tongue.

Every day, something new: columbine
dark pink and intricate. Your eyes meeting
mine in the mirror. The yellow-black design
of black-hooded garter snakes heating

themselves in remains of Russian Sage.
The crabapple blooming. A pink and splendid rage.

Shanan Ballam

DEAR MARCY

in the wetlands
this morning
a flock
of ibis glides
ebony.

I miss you.

I always knew it would
happen,

but I wasn't prepared
for it to be so
soon.

We were just texting
last night with Al.
It was the 10-year
anniversary of Dylan's
death.

You had just had your shoulder replaced.
You told us you had been
diagnosed with primary progressive
Multiple sclerosis.

I told you I saw a monarch
butterfly and things would be okay.

We were supposed to go to lunch
the next day.

I hope you aren't in pain anymore.
I hope you died in your sleep
because of a drop
in your blood pressure.

Al has seen three monarch
butterflies since you died.

A swallowtail thumped
its lovely body
against the window.

I think it was you,
telling me you're okay.

I went to bed so I didn't see your
last text:

I have 2 yellow and black monarchs that come every day.
I could watch them forever.

Shanan Ballam is a Senior Lecturer at Utah State University where she teaches poetry writing and composition. She had a stroke that paralyzed her entire right side and robbed her of language. She is the author of three poetry collections and the forthcoming chapbook *first poems after the stroke*. These poems won honorable mention in The Love Book Contest of Blue Cedar Press.

WE DO NOT LOVE EACH OTHER

Your skin is like red yarrow blooming
under wax paper, which is like how
we love each other.

The word love, as in the tongue meeting the teeth, the
teeth meeting the lip, is not like
how we love each other.

We do not love each other like kneading bread,
like digging our fingernails into the earth, like a
dog tears open a rabbit.

We temper our coffee with milk and
honey.

We do not love each other like the vast bright
silence,
like the sting of white sun on blue snow.

Our love is soft, our love is for the
weekends, is a blanket folded in a square,
is evening the batter in a pan, is patting the
soil smooth.

Julia Bindler lives in Minneapolis where she recently participated in
The Loft's poetry apprenticeship program. Her work has appeared
in *ONE ART.*

HOW DO I KNOW?

By a welcome uplifting presence
By a breath of original air
By a sustained exceptional note

By a gentle constancy of current
By a familiar simplicity of music
By a freely expanding compass

By a resonant thrill in my body
By a harmonious sound in my soul
By a clear tenor in my spirit

By all of these, I know
She is the one.

Cammie Funston

MOON RIVER THEATRE

I turn and catch your profile
In the halo of the stage lights,
Your features relaxed,
Your smile soft and natural.

I am compelled to keep shifting my gaze
Back and forth,
From the seasoned, sequined crooners,
To your joy-washed face.

What good fortune for me
To have been invited here,
The ring-side seat on your right
Where I can keep vigil.

Delight is a spirited dancer
Perfecting her moves
In the mirrors of your eyes,
And I her most devoted fan.

For the rest of my life, it will be my pleasure,
To clap her into being,
And whenever I catch her preening
In those boyish blues

My soul will sing ovations,
And my heart will leap to its feet
And shout, "Bravo!" and "Encore!"
Just to see her dancing in your eyes again.

Cammie Funston

NEW YEAR'S DAY

I dreamt you followed me
down a corridor of snow into the light.

In the blinding dawn
I heard the familiar fall of your feet, steady in the distance.

When I faltered, you paused.
At the crystal clearing

I sensed you, true as being, calmly breathing,
close enough to kiss the back of my neck.

Cammie Funston, a native of Wichita, Kansas, holds a BS in Human Resources Management from Friends University and a BA in Communication Sciences and Disorders from Wichita State University. A retired educator, Cammie enjoys hand-building pottery and is an advocate for persons with intellectual and developmental disabilities.

HOW FAR CAN YOU GO TO SUSTAIN LOVE?

Sally Timmel

Waiting in an airport for my beloved partner to arrive became routine over the forty-six years of our trans-national relationship.

We met at Boston University's Master degree program where we both were told to look out for each other by mutual friends. I was not interested in befriending a white South African. I had served in the Peace Corps in Ethiopia and returned to the USA to work with Black leaders on civil rights. I told myself I would be civil but did not want to befriend a white South African. Within days of our meeting, however, I was falling in love with Anne Hope.

One month after we met Anne wrote:

Surprised by Passion

Reflections on a Monday morning
Who is this Sally?
Who can she be?
with her laughter and pain
and vitality,
with her honest exposure –
so fearless to risk and
her genuine acceptance
of rind and of husk.
so piercingly truthful
compellingly glad
calling forth meanings
that never I had
opening a door
into firelight and flame
dancing with politics

knowledge a game
ready to share
death, doubt and fear
and linking of neurons
from any old where.
What's in her chemistry,
What's in her blood,
that causes a rainbow
to rise from the mud.
How You did make her,
and how You did shake her,
how You did love her
and cause her to be....
What all do You mean
with this bright gift to me.
(October 1969)

Soon we were working together in Boston leading anti-racism workshops for white groups. Together we developed participatory methods that worked well to enable participants to see how institutional racism was deeply entrenched in both of our countries.

After we graduated, Anne's visa expired, and she returned to South Africa. I was on the apartheid government's list of *personas non grata*, not allowed to enter South Africa because of my anti-apartheid activism. Not wanting to be apart, Anne found me a job in neighboring Swaziland.

Anne was working with Steve Biko, founder of the Black Consciousness Movement and later murdered by the apartheid government. Steve Biko said that "the impact of these workshops [with Anne] was so profound that they changed the outlook of the Black Consciousness members." (Cited in a new book by Biko's son, Hlumelo Biko, *Black Consciousness: A Love Story*). A number of Black Consciousness members were arrested, and Anne was told that she would be also or would have to go into exile. One day the police came to her office and demanded her passport. Anne told them her passport was at home and the police drove her to her house. They did not ask her for directions and walked straight to her bedroom where she kept her passport, demonstrating that they had had her under surveillance. She chose to flee South Africa and live in exile.

We worked together in Kenya doing training through the churches for the next seven years, and then took a one-year sabbatical in the US. Next Anne traveled to Zimbabwe where she had family. And I moved to Cincinnati, Ohio to work on a political campaign, not wanting to leave the U.S. Our separation was hard, and I moved back to Africa to be with Anne. Kenya had been independent for 10 years, and the rich were thriving in that capitalist country. But Zimbabweans had just won majority rule and expected the new government would immediately respond to the needs of the poor majority, not the rich.

Anne found me work in a literacy-adult education program, but I was unhappy and felt stifled. We argued for months, and I applied for jobs in the USA. but did not find work. My experiences overseas seemed not to fit the criteria. Eventually Anne found a job in Washington, D.C. so that we could be together. Being exiled from her homeland had been a major sacrifice. Now she was leaving Africa, another sacrifice.

Anne worked with a Catholic think-tank and I was hired as the legislative director for Church Women United. Anne found the consumerism and politics in the United States very difficult to live with. She became depressed, while I was in my glory, organizing grassroots groups and working with others in the religious community on foreign policy issues and to cut military spending. We began therapy both together and separately. I needed help understanding the tremendous toll exile takes. I didn't know how to deal with her depression. So I fell in love with another woman and left Anne. That new relationship enabled me to discover more of who I was and that I needed to find my own path; I was too co-dependent on Anne.

Anne wrote the following poem at that time:

Why?

For thirteen years my heart was still
round and whole and strong.
Sometimes glad and sometimes sad,
hardening now and then,
but mostly
warm,
responsive, calm,
resilient and firm.
Then
suddenly
the thing went mad
turned somersaults of glee
sent orange darts across the sky
in serendipity
The world grew young and beautiful.
Hope blossomed like an imp.
Then everything was possible,
no change too hard to choose
Sun shone inside from being known
no fear that I might lose.
And why should all this simply fade
as daylight leaves the sky
and grey replace the golden glow.
My heart keeps asking……….
Why?

By then things were changing in South Africa. The South African economy was collapsing as sanctions and divestment had a major impact. Trade unions and churches had coalesced, all of that together with the ANC's armed resistance to apartheid causing major disruptions and forcing change. After twenty-seven years in prison Nelson Mandela was released in 1991 and negotiated with the white-minority apartheid government a transition to majority rule in which all South Africans would able to vote equally for a new government. Ann could finally return to her homeland!

At the same time, the woman I had fallen in love with found someone else and a friend of Anne's found a job for her at the University of Cape Town.

Before returning to South Africa, Anne gave workshops in the Philippines. I located the number of her return flight and met her at the airport. She was quite cool to me, but after a few months allowed me back to the house we owned together. A few days before my 50th birthday, Anne left for Cape Town.

For the next four years I remained in Washington doing work I loved and went to Cape Town to be with Anne for three or four months each year. I was not sure that our relationship could survive the combination of my deception and the distance that separated us. We struggled with how and where we might be together. Anne took me to wonderful places on the Atlantic and Indian Ocean coasts that were paradises. But being productive was important to me and I was leery of having no work I could pour myself into. At the same time, I knew that being with Anne was essential. From the States, I called Anne to say I would move there indefinitely. Anne wrote this poem at that time:

Joy, joy, joy in the morning

Tired after a great fight
wrestling all night with grief…
and, in the morning,

a voice on the telephone saying, "Yes!
Let's give it another chance"
My heart begins to dance.
A feastday breakfast –
fragrance of coffee and bacon
filling the house with smells of happy days.
Fried eggs and orange juice,
toast and marmalade
sitting in the sunshine of a blue, blue day.
Brahms double concerto, drumming a dance of joy .
A plunge in the pool, singing, with Christina Rosetti,
"My heart is like a singing bird,
whose nest is in a watered shoot.
My heart is like an apple tree,
whose boughs are hung with thick-set fruit
My heart is like a rainbow shell,
that paddles in a halcyon sea,
My heart is gladder than all these,
because my love will come to me."
(October 1991)

In 1993, we bought a house that overlooked the Indian Ocean
and the back of Table Mountain. We now knew our future would
be together. With an Iranian economist teaching at the University
of Cape Town we started an economic literacy program to train
activists how to read government budgets and lobby for funds
for local needs. I raised money fulltime and had a purpose while
Anne thrived training women. After five years, together Anne
and I founded a training center for local community development
programs and job training.

In 2001, our methods for training local people were published as *Training for Transformation*. We drew together five women to plan a one-year training program that we would offer internationally, found an institute in Ireland to accredit this program, wrote a funding proposal, and by 2002 had recruited 40 participants from 11 countries to participate at our training center near Cape Town. By 2020, over 61 countries were implementing this work with much success using our books. We facilitated a one-year diploma course in Training for Transformation, each of us leading different weeks of the training

Anne had always supported my work. After she retired she became very involved in spiritual direction, meditations, and hiking the mountains surrounding Cape Town with new friends. We were on different paths, but mutually supportive. No more co-dependency for either of us.

In 2014, we moved to a retirement community in South California where we had long time friends. Anne died of cancer a year and a half later. Leaving her country this final time was a wonderful last gift Anne gave me. I miss her every day.

International love relationships face unique issues like, Which country to live in? and, Can either partner get legal papers to live in a country other than their own?

But our love survived and still does, I think because we faced in the same direction. When we first met in 1969, we went to a dance and watched three sets of couples dancing. The first couple danced separately, facing different directions and coming together sometimes. A second couple danced close together all of the time. The third couple danced closely at times, not always touching but facing the same direction. After that dance, Anne said to me, "We are that third couple."

When we celebrated 40 years together, Anne read from a book written by South African Olive Schreiner in the 1890's, *A Track to the Water's Edge:* "This story tells of a young woman searching for the land of freedom, who meets an old wise woman on the banks of a deep and dangerous river. The old woman, Reason, advises her that to get to the land of freedom, she must go down the banks of labor, through the waters of suffering, setting aside her 'cloak of ancient received opinions' and the 'shoes of dependence' on her feet. The young woman asks if many have crossed before and is told that many have tried. She is reminded of the locusts, some of which tried to cross and were heard of no more. 'Heard of no more?' the young woman exclaims horrified. 'Heard of no more,' Reason repeats. 'But what of that? With their bodies they have built a bridge over which many more could pass. They made a track to the water's edge!' "

Anne said, "We have chosen this theme because we do hope that, with our [Training for Transformation] books and all the work we have done, and the work of many others, some of whom 'are heard of no more,' we have helped to make 'a track to the water's edge,' contributing to the building of a bridge, which can be used for those who are truly seeking the 'land of freedom.'"

We loved and persevered for 46 years together! Perhaps Jesuit Superior General Arrupe said it best:

What you are in love with,

What seizes your imagination,

Will affect everything.

It will decide what will get you out of bed in the morning,

What you do with your evenings,

How you spend your weekend,

What you read, who you know,

What breaks your heart,

And what amazes you with joy and gratitude.

Fall in love,

Stay in love,

And it will decide everything.

Sally Timmel grew up in a small town in Wisconsin and attended a Methodist women's college. In 1962, the first year of the Peace Corps, she, with three African Americans, worked as a Peace Corps volunteer in Ethiopia. Sally and Anne's published auto/biographies are: *ANNE HOPE, the Struggle for Freedom: The Life of the Visionary Co-Founder of Training for Transformation* by Stephanie Kilroe and *You Can Never Go Back: The Autobiography of the Co-Founder of the Grail Conference and Retreat Centre and Training for Transformation* by Sally Timmel.

SHOWER

I meditate on showering with you.
Life immemorial, days evolving, bookend the moment.
Relived in contemplative replay,
we soap, rinse each other, press our dimorphism together.
These palms belong to your
toned, petite, shapely shape, shaped by quotidian doing.
Mouthing, deeply inhaling auburn locks, proceeding.
Under a hot-water onslaught, breathe deep again, after
shampooing, that rustiness clings to nape and shoulders.

Totality I have clung to from our dramatic beginning:
Toes-feet-ankles-shins-calves-knees-thighs converge
on your *Bermuda Triangle*: jeopardy, spattering water,
faint radio static, all search parties call it quits, dial then
turned off, towel now thrown in.
Done, you make up my mind, instantly: doubtless I'll get
old only with you, or so I think
at the drain's last complaint: a given, taken away before
giving it any thought; stepping out.

Tom Gannon Hamilton

STILL HERE

Decades wave goodbye; you're still here
and I'm clueless why our dots overlap on this
vast pointillist canvas,
paired grace-notes in the grand human fugue.
Those around us know at a glance what we'd
only deny if asked outright.

So they tease, intimating intimacy beyond
your scope or mine; our actual searing
topography, dermal inferno, these burning
capillaries, nearby glades might mollify: cool
sanctuary neither you nor I have ever found.

So novel that we scan the embarrassed ground
rather than each other's downcast
eyelash-embossed faces; flushed,
speechless but for the plan to rendezvous.

Dockside, a chance reflection, subdued shock
to see myself with you, then through
tea-hued water we drift in afternoon's canoe.

You've taken fore, I'm aft; between dips,
from time to time, pausing here, here
and here, while the paddle drips.
I'll reassure myself you're palpable
as the nude, glacier-scoured, granite shelf
onto which we lift: you the bow, me the stern.

Breath-warm-wind-mussed-acanthus-tousle;
uncertain where mine end, yours begin.
Our skin: single tan crayon
from the same unopened carton, on the cusp
of polychrome Autumn.

August bids us recline; fingers tame divine
locks, your satin cheek, chin my palm cups,
kept on my breast half-a-century; still here.

Tom Gannon Hamilton

I DEAL

for Donna

You feel bookish; by pure happy happenstance
here, outside, the atmosphere is room temperature.
Gooseflesh-inducing, a freshet
arrives, then leaves
rustle, a bit soporific, the way two camomile teabags
nestle, infusing evening.
I speculate on such optimistic optics, deal in ideals:
eye-deals, bargain images, economic
visions purchased on sight for what it cost me to see.

I'm done with hashtags, personal causes
and special effects pretty much lost on the rabble.
Ignore the nervous many, forget about frenetic they.
It is time to quit parroting scary oration.
Let us pay profiteering doom babble no more heed.
Focus on art, mine, yours: collaborative, affirmative,
heartfelt, phonetic our, spelt *oh you are*
she who engages, when combined with me, so
together that we're one another's reward.

You gather what I've gathered: how all writing leans

toward revision, as any

speech earning a hearing means translation, I need

your touch at each reading,

whether my book sits up or is reclined, its inviting

back and front cover:

upper and lower lips, thin yet kind,

while behind them, white, mischievous pages grin.

Turning now, you look, returning the smile.

Tom Gannon Hamilton is published in *Dalhousie*, *Vallum* (Canada), *Lummox* (California), *Verse & Voice* (Hong King), *Voices* (Israel), *inScribe* (Australia), and *Amsterdam Quarterly* (Netherlands). He won first prizes for "El Marillo" (2018) in the *Big Pond Rumours* Chapbook Competition and "Non-Consultant" (2021) in the *Love Lies Bleeding* Contest. His books include *Panoptic* (2018), *The Mezzo Soprano Dines Alone* (2021), and *To Grace Bridges* (2023) from Aeolus House.

OPENING

to love

A sweetness in the eyes that can't be forced

created the connection
from the start

Smiling eyes a soft liking, fondness
settling like
a gentle exhale
a rest
a closed-mouthed grin

and the eyes that spoke it all from the beginning.

Reconnecting to it now

I feel calm
still
safe
and content

It's always there
under it all
to be connected with

because it was never lost and never will be

Because it's you
connecting with me

i feel it
and the energy flows
Inhale
Exhale

Soon there's no telling between the two

And we're here again
now
like we've never left
time hasn't passed
Because the love is always there

Tara Ryan is a graduate of Skidmore College and the Institute for Integrative Nutrition, originally from Sandy Hook, CT. She is a creative content consultant who loves supporting visionaries in bringing their dreams into form. She is a board-certified health coach.

TO SAY YES

And shall the full weight of your yes
embrace you,
   buoy you,
      melt into you
         like warm butter
         on an english muffin
      while your greasy chin
      smiles?

And have your unmatched
threads and rough edges become
   the compost for
      tomatoes
      succulent and
      ripe
            in the long light?

And will you inhale
every moment of that light,
   even as the days shorten
          and the comb fills
        like the rising flame of your *yes*?

- for Maria & Paul on their wedding day

Kathy Whitham

DRAWING THE BIG DIPPER

Like a garter snake's hollow skin in the yard,

thoughts tumble through a windowpane,

letters separating from words.

My bare feet in the sun

plump and ready to sweeten your breath.

There's more room under the wide than the narrow.

The curve of your top lip

beside the embering wood stove.

Like lying on a warm slab of coastal granite,

breath stunned by a mass of silent stars.

In the warm pocket of our blanket burrow

I draw the Big Dipper

along the contour of your waist and hip,

my fingertips tuned to your answer.

Kathy Whitham

I COULD ALMOST BELIEVE LOVE

I could almost believe love, out of miscellaneous detritus,

rises all at once, like pigeons in a city park.

Rushing to the naked, powerful taste of dark fruit.

An insistent sunrise tearing open the dawn

with pink feathered wings.

In a rose petalled bra

and ruby red stilettos,

I quaff coffee from a cup

the color of a turned-on tomato.

Kathy Whitham, an active member of the Boston writing community and a Parenting Coach for non-traditional families, explores myriad forms of human connection in her poetry. She recently finalized a chapbook collection, "Drawing The Big Dipper." Her work appeared in *what the poem knows, A tribute to Barbara Helfgott Hyett.*

LOVE KNOWS NO

Love knows no boundaries of division,

no dividing lines of culture and religion

no guarded borders between sovereign nations,

no gradation of skin pigmentations,

no gender differences or generations.

Like Romeo and Juliet

of Montague and Capulet

or Tony and Maria

of the rumbling West Side Sharks and Jets,

The only thing love might regret

when two foreign hearts connect

is the fact that still as yet

it's easy for some people to reject

and hard for others to accept.

James Fly

GIVE LOVE ANOTHER CHANCE

Give love another chance:

Dare to rekindle romance.

Don't let the past

be your final dance.

Take that special someone by their hands

and kick up your heels and prance.

Give love another chance!

James Fly

BODY AND SOUL

You can't fall in love with a body.

You can only fall in love with a soul.

It's okay to appreciate

but a body will deteriorate

as time and life take their toll.

But a person's essence,

their immaculate presence,

stays forever young and whole.

How long will it take until we know

you can admire a body

but only love a soul?

James Fly graduated from Pacific Union College, Angwin, California with a degree in journalism and served in public relations and development for Walla Walla College (now University), Walla Walla, WA., and Conception Abbey Seminary College in Northwest Missouri. He is the author of three books of poetry, *Zenphoniquely, Patighette,* and *Evolving* published by Amazing Things Press. He is semi-retired and helps manage a new age book and gift shop in Livingston, Montana.

STRAY

You come to my door like a stray dog.

Your tail between your legs and your heart in your hand.

And though I know better, I still let you in.

I wish I could escape this hold you have on me.

But you still have that same stupid smile

And coffee-colored eyes that feel like home.

With each white lie, you pull me back in again.

As I begin to hope, I can turn the stray into a companion.

Telling myself we'll stick this time.

I try to cherish the good times.

All our laughter and midnight dances in the kitchen.

I hold onto it like the faded picture of us from when we were kids,

With your buck teeth and my scraped knees.

But I know how this ends.

We'll eventually wake up from this spell.

You'll return to the alleyways again,

And I'll wish we had just stayed friends.

Adalyn Waeltermann

LOVE'S SLOW BLOOM

His love came in like the spring sun,
A slow-moving soft warmth.
Brought forth by his bright sage-colored eyes.

Days spent together with butterflies in our stomachs,
Encapsulated in bright watercolor memories.
Memories that would replace the coldness of winter.

With each warm breeze between us,
With each gentle clasp of our hands and that bright smile,
He made the dormant orchid that was my heart begin to bloom.

Adalyn Waeltermann

THE LEFTOVERS OF LOVE

This is what you don't recover from.

The ever-present remnants of love.

Like leftover bullet shards that never got taken out.

Years will pass, and the memories still leave you numb.

Just when I think I'm over it, someone will say your name.

Forcing images of you to cloud my brain.

How your eyes were dark brown pools that seemed

    to always overflow.

Because no matter the situation, you always took the blame.

Then, there'll be the memories that feel like a warm blanket.

Soft and golden, like the single bleached strand hidden

    in your brown hair.

The days when your laugh would bounce off the walls

    without a care.

These memories fill me with an overwhelming urge to call you.

But I never actually do.

Adalyn Waeltermann is a college student at the University of Kansas and an aspiring writer.

THE STORM

Gretchen Cassel Eick

Late December 2023. The Washington, D.C. office of Children's International occupied a three-story brownstone near Capitol Hill. The taxi driver clicked the release on his trunk so she could retrieve her two bags. He didn't help her lug her suitcases up the flight of stairs to the entrance. It had begun to rain with a vengeance and the lowered sky threatened a major storm.

She rang the bell and waited, then rang again, her coat peppered with rain spots. She felt water sliding down her cheeks, dripping from her nose, her hair. She held a newspaper over her head and prayed they were open this early.

Eventually, an older woman who introduced herself as Sally opened the door and invited her in.

"I'm Priscilla Musleh. I'm just returned from Gaza to bring you my report," she said in a rush, still awed that she had made it out at all.

"Oh, yes! Welcome. You must be exhausted. And you're all wet! Wait in here while I'll fetch a towel." Sally ushered her to a small waiting room. "Would you like a cup of coffee or tea?"

"Yes, please. Coffee. With sugar, no cream."

Sally returned in a few minutes with towels and coffee. "I'll find Mr. Kovich and let him know you're here. I'm afraid tonight is our big fund raiser, so things are rather hectic. We're worried the storm may cut into our attendance." Smiling, Sally hurried away down the hall.

Sinking into a chair, Priscilla opened her roller bag, retrieved a dry pair of socks and shoes, and rubbed her hair dry with the towel. Closing her eyes, she listened to the sounds of the building — footsteps on the bare wood floors, clicking computer keys, voices on the telephones, and the rain that muted every sound. She felt she was in a kind of echo chamber.

She was exhausted. And depressed. As discouraged as she had ever felt in her entire life.

After twenty minutes Mr. Kovich entered the room. He was about her age, fifty-ish, and his face appeared care-worn. His hair stood up, probably from his nervous habit of repeatedly running his fingers across his scalp. It gave him a surprised look.

"Ms. Musleh? I'm terribly sorry to have kept you waiting. I had forgotten you were coming today. We're rather overwhelmed with preparations for tonight. How was your trip?"

She didn't speak of her flight, only of the children's hospital the Israelis had bombed and the orphanage beside her mother-in-law's home that had run out of blankets, medicine, electricity, and food.

She rooted in her carryall and brought out an envelope with the photos she had taken. It pleased her how interested and attentive he was, asking for details and making notes. He appeared genuinely distressed by the suffering her photos recorded — children half covered with rubble or wrapped in shrouds for burial, old people weeping as they huddled beside the one remaining wall of their home, mass graves in the yard of the hospital, young male survivors, digging for signs of life. These nine weeks she had wondered if anyone cared. The destruction of innocents intensified daily, yet the media coverage made it sound like the people of Gaza had an army and sophisticated weapons, like they were a match for their attackers.

In fact, Gaza was no bigger than a moderate U.S. city and enclosed by Israeli-built walls; no Palestinians could get out and supplies could not get in due to Israel's war on Gaza that had begun in early October. Sometimes the despair that weighed her down made everything she saw the monochromatic grays of bombed buildings.

Thunder and then loud cracks of lightning interrupted their conversation while he studied her report, taking time he had told her he didn't have today.

"Working in a war zone is terribly difficult. You've done well. And I'm sure it has taken its toll on you. I am so sorry...Are you staying in D.C. long?" His eyes held hers.

"No, I have a plane to catch to Chicago this afternoon at four. My mother is waiting for me there and quite anxious, as you can understand," she replied.

"If the storm is as bad as they're predicting, your flight may be canceled," he cautioned. "You're welcome to stay here. One advantage of renting an old brownstone for our office space is we have a room with a bath upstairs. And a cot."

She thought he seemed to be a caring person. She felt a rush of gratitude for his kindness.

When Beethoven's 5th sounded from his phone, he stood and extended his hand. "I'm afraid I must go attend to more details for tonight. Are you comfortable waiting here until you leave for Reagan Airport?"

At her nod, he left the room and hurried up the stairs.

A short while later Sally returned. She asked how Priscilla had become an aid worker and listened carefully.

"My husband was from Palestine — from Gaza." Priscilla's words were labored. "We met in Chicago while we were both in grad school studying journalism... After we married, we stayed in the U.S... We tried for years to have children, but I miscarried six times."

She turned her wedding ring round and round her finger. This was not easy to talk about. She took a deep breath and plunged on. "He went back to visit his family in 2016, just before Israel invaded Gaza, and was killed there. We think he was targeted as a journalist. If I had not found meaningful employment, my grief would have buried me. I contacted a number of nonprofit organizations working in the region and you all hired me." She tried to look appreciative.

"I was in the north of Gaza visiting my husband's family when Hamas raided Israel October 7th, followed immediately by the Israeli assault on Gaza. I couldn't get out for nine weeks. Gaza is walled and the Israeli Defense Forces would not allow anyone to leave. I tried to report on what I saw and heard. I guess I am lucky that I wasn't one of the forty-seven journalists killed."

She looked carefully at Sally. Had she said too much?

"Please go on," Sally urged.

"My husband's family live in the north, Gaza City, the area Israel demanded be evacuated, so we experienced the full force of the invasion. We had to flee their home to escape the bombing and to find food and water…."

Priscilla had been talking so fast she was out of breath. She had carried what was happening in Palestine inside her and urgently needed to talk about it. When you covered war zones, you made a conscious effort to summarize, consolidate your words, abbreviate to hold the horror at bay. She worried she had already stretched Sally's capacity to take it all in.

"I got out four days ago through the Rafah crossing, the only way one can get out. I caught a flight to Washington so I could deliver to you my report and my photos. I knew you all would hear my story even if no one else believed me."

Sally studied Priscilla's devastated face in silence before touching the woman's hand. She meant it as a gesture of sympathy. Her face was soft and her eyes tender.

"Mr. Kovich has a similar story. This work is his salvation, too."

Hail pounding on the window drew their eyes to the storm outside this cozy sanctuary. Sally appeared suddenly distracted.

"That sounds worrisome. We have put a lot of money into tonight's fundraiser, but who will come if it is storming like this? Anyway, let me take you to our room upstairs where you can have a nap or at least be more comfortable."

Sally picked up Priscilla's roller bag and led the way upstairs to a back room with a single bed and an overstuffed chair. Through a door Priscilla could see a small bathroom.

"Mr. Kovich stays here some nights," Sally said.

Priscilla's phone binged. It was a text from United Airlines. "Oh, no! My flight was canceled!"

"I'm sorry. Let me get some blankets and towels so you can settle in. It will be all right. This isn't a bad place to ride out the storm."

Alone, Priscilla opened her bags and took out her belongings, savoring the memories they brought of Ali's family. She pushed away the other, horrific memories that crowded her brain. Rain-sound made time stand still.

Mr. Kovich appeared in the doorway. "Sally tells me your flight was canceled. Please do stay with us. There is food and you can attend our fund raiser — both to enjoy the catered meal… and pad our attendance numbers!" He smiled warmly.

He paused and then stepped into the room, studying her closely.

"Sally told me your story. I'm very sorry. One wonders if one's grief will ever end."

His kindness and the sadness on his face made her want very much for it to end for him. And for her. She replied: "People tell me there comes a time when we are surprised by joy again. But we have to wait for it. We can't push the river."

His face lit with recognition. "C. S. Lewis! That book has brought me through many long nights. You, too, it seems."

She nodded.

"You wonder why you are still here in the face of so much loss and suffering. You don't know what to do. Grief numbs you." He looked at her to see if she understood.

Eyes wet she mumbled, "Yes."

In that moment something changed.

As they shared the pain of their solitude and isolation, the pain of overwhelming losses, the possibility of new life opened before them. Simultaneously. They smiled. She asked him about his life, and he talked while time passed.

Thirty minutes later they noticed that the storm seemed to be subsiding.

Sally knocked on the door jamb. "NPR just announced that planes are flying again from Reagan. Check your airline. Perhaps you can get to Chicago after all."

Priscilla pulled out her phone and entered her flight number in the United app.

Mr. Kovich knelt to help refill her suitcases. His eyes avoided hers. She could feel the warmth of his body beside hers as together they restored her belongings to her bag. He smelled pleasantly of Ivory soap.

She closed her phone.

He looked at her, questioning.

'Maybe I should stay?" she said, looking up from packing.

She closed her half-packed bag and took a deep breath, her voice soft and tentative. "One thing I learned in the past nine weeks: life is short and you can't count on tomorrow. I'll never find joy again if I can't risk being wrong. Perhaps this could be that time."

Mr. Kovich simply beamed.

Gretchen Cassel Eick is a world traveler and professor of history who has five published novels and two prize-winning histories, *Dissent in Wichita: The Civil Rights Movement in the Midwest, 1954-72* (University of Illinois Press) and *They Met at Wounded Knee: The Eastmans' Story* (University of Nevada Press). This story was published in the Winter 2023-24 issue of *The Write Bridge Literary Journal* (Anamcara Press).

INTIMATIONS OF MOUNT HARVARD:

THE STORY OF THE PARENT/CHILD, CONTIGUOUS UNITED STATES FIVE HIGHEST TOPS

Doug Emory

A year ago, I authored an article poking fun at mountaineers' penchant for applying mathematical calculations to every imaginable aspect of the sport. As a quick illustration of this odd proclivity, two speakers at a convocation I attended recently both used scattergrams, graphed onto Cartesian coordinate systems, to illustrate their decades-long compilation of climbing achievements.

I'm guilty of this approach as anyone. There I'll be, traversing under an azure sky, surrounded by iridescent snowfields and soaring rock faces, utterly oblivious because I'm busily calculating my elevation gain per hour and my target summit's placement on scales of topographic isolation and prominence.

This is sick behavior, so several years back I resolved to return to my pre-peak-bagging, Romantic roots. I wandered river valleys. I plucked wildflowers and hearkened to bird song. I breathed deep the air.

I was horrifically bored. After my years chasing quixotic numerical goals, my efforts at a Wordsworthian rebirth failed to blossom. This outcome has left me with a guilty dissatisfaction that I'm loathe to subject to a searching and fearless examination, but one point has emerged with crystalline clarity: my addiction to STEM-adjacent mountaineering is unshakeable. And nothing illustrates this affliction more than my pursuit of a challenge of my own invention--climbing the Contiguous United States, Five Highest Tops, all with my beleaguered son Nathan in tow.

You can be forgiven fuzziness about the Five Highest Tops. Summiting the group is a fanciful activity recognized by few, like pickleball or half the sports currently in the Olympic Games. I myself chanced upon this quest like a person beginning a hike down an unmarked trail, only to emerge in a clearing where a neon signpost flashed: "Man, you are on to *Something*!" Then I personalized the journey, upping the level of difficulty by requiring Nathan to pose atop each peak beside me, despite his petulant attempts at living a somewhat normal existence of his own.

In order, the Five Highest are:
• California's Mount Whitney at 14,505 feet
• Colorado's Mts. Elbert (14,440); Massive (14,428);
  and Harvard (14,420)
• My own Washington State's Mount Rainier at 14,411

The tale of our fifteen-year struggle to attain the Parent/Child, Contiguous U.S. Five Highest Tops is worthy of consideration, for two reasons. First, for those wilderness enthusiasts and outdoor adventurers out there, the mountains are sublime. Secondly, the undertaking works as a stress test of the bonds between parents and children, illuminating these complex and often disquieting relationships. In my family's case, I love Nathan, heart and soul, but he maintains a belief I conned him into mountaineering, lying pathologically about the traumas implicit in this lifestyle. Anytime I now use standard phrases like, "It's right around the next bend." or "It's just over this false summit," my words are met with derisive laughter.

Truth is, Nathan brought his involvement in peak-bagging on himself. As a toddler, he could have pitched a tantrum on the trail. Instead, he marched doggedly forward. By age four, he'd appeared in a local paper, described as a boy who could out-climb and out-talk the average adult. At age seven, he made his first roped winter ascent and at ten traversed a glacier and hopped his first crevasse. Soon after turning fifteen, he announced his desire to be the first student in his high school to scale Mount Rainier.

Unbeknownst to us then, that 2007 Rainier assault began our expedition toward the Five Highest Tops. Rainier is the hardest of these climbs, the only one with technical requirements. It's also a tricky mountain, no more than a hard workout in good conditions but, at worst, impossible. This realization surfaced all the pitfalls of my bipolar parenting style. Initially, I swelled with pride. The triumphant photo of father and son posed atop Rainier showed so vividly in my mind I could have picked out the frame. I pooh-poohed the mountain's inherent dangers. Then, as our departure day neared, a knee-weakening terror gripped me.

Frantically, I enlisted four of my climbing partners to shelter my baby from harm, protecting him on the rope's either end. They enthusiastically agreed, but, unfortunately, they then performed with their usual reliability. One dropped out the night before and, without consulting us, signed on a non-climber in his place. Two others arrived at the Paradise Lodge hours late, suffering from terminal alcohol poisoning. As we slugged up the Muir Snowfield, they repeatedly yodeled Nathan back so they could shift items from their packs to his.

My debilitated friends abandoned us at Camp Muir, and our surviving team of four started for the top after sunup, hours after the recommended time for beginning summit day. Altitude sickness repeatedly struck our novice team member, but, impressively, he kept shuffling forward, only pausing to vomit on his boots. Our pace, to coin a phrase, became glacial. In mid-afternoon, we tagged the top while the snow bridges below us softened dangerously. I shouted myself hoarse, urging my team to hurry each time Nathan crossed a crevasse, precariously balanced on an impossibly fragile arch of snow. After a grueling twenty-hour day, we finally reached the car, with hallucinations haunting each of us from the shadows.

In reflecting on this fiasco, I at first blamed my sorry group of friends. Later, more objectively, it became evident my judgment and conditioning were equally suspect. In a couple of photos, Nathan sits, arm wrapped around his ice ax, looking like a little boy some fool has dropped onto a steeply canted glacier. In many others, he's a strapping young adult, one who could have been a Patagonia gear model but for being regrettably yoked to me, a wheezing geezer. My helmet perches like an inverted tulip on my head. I vaguely resemble a soldier of Gondor, one of those nameless LOTR extras marching off to get bludgeoned by orcs.

The following September, with Nathan still in high school and thus still at the mercy of my vacation scheduling, we jetted to Vegas and drove across Death Valley, heading for a campsite at Whitney Portal. Our goal was Mount Whitney, twenty-two miles and six thousand feet of elevation from our tents. We hiked by headlamp through pine forest and then above tree line. The sun set Wotan's Throne and the surrounding palisades aflame with liquid fire while the air held still as glass.

At Trail Camp Pond, we wolfed snacks, ascended to the cables, and hiked the ninety-nine switchbacks—which I naturally counted to ensure mathematical accuracy. We topped out at Trail Crest then pressed beyond the junction with the John Muir Trail. Over those last miles, Nathan suffered from altitude sickness, so much so I worried he might turn back. But, as he'd done from toddler days, he persevered. We strode past the summit hut and onto Whitney's vast rocky summit, Muir's range of light spread in glory around us.

That gave us two of the five, the hardest and the highest, but my burning bush vision of the Five Highest Tops didn't hit till six years later, after Nathan graduated college and I stole a few days from work.

In 2014, we set off to Colorado's Sawatch Range, home to over a dozen enormous, lumpy fourteen-thousand-foot peaks — known affectionately in the state as Fourteeners. We arrived not even having set our targets, knowing we only had two days to climb. For whatever mysterious reason, Mount Massive became our Day One objective. We charged up the six-mile trail, the weather perfect, a deep blue sky etched with horsetail clouds. We were alone on the mountain, just the two of us chattering as we crossed the silent tundra of Massive's eastern slopes. At a saddle near 14,000 feet, we gained the final ridge. The wind chuffed at us then built into an unrelenting blast. We lost the trail, scrambled a spiked crown of shattered rock, and then our route rematerialized below. Soon after, we grabbed a scrap of cardboard scrawled in magic marker and snapped a selfie with it held under our chins—Mount Massive, 14, 421 ft.

That afternoon, we stopped at a Chinese restaurant in Leadville. Tellingly, we were the only customers, but we barely noticed. We were starving. Our egg drop soup included wilted lettuce leaves and the kitchen's every spare can of mixed vegetables. The chef plopped down at a table nearby, staring at us, as if evaluating whether hungry climbers would indeed eat anything.

I paid him little mind because a plan was burbling in my subconscious. That evening, over beers in a Vail bar, it burst forth formed fully as Athena from Zeus' forehead. At home I had numbered logs of my highest peaks. I had counts not just of Colorado Fourteeners but of every trip above 14,000 feet. I charted my progress on Washington State's Homecourt and Backcourt 100 lists. But now I'd discovered something better, something unique to my son and me. We had one climb left before returning to Seattle. Holy Cross, I informed Nathan, was off the list. So was Huron. Did he realize our little team had summited the first, third and fifth highest peaks in the contiguous US? Did he understand we were embarked on a grand journey toward the Parent/Child Contiguous U.S. Five Highest Tops?

Of course he didn't. He's more or less sane. But, next morning, he rose and trudged with me up the gigantic blob of Mt. Elbert. Unhappy high school teachers and their grumbling charges littered the featureless trail. On the summit ridge snow fell and a Cascade-quality whiteout shrouded the top. We dug another of those cardboard signs from a snowdrift — Mount Elbert, 14,440 feet — snapped our selfie and headed down. Dull it assuredly was, but Elbert was Colorado's highest peak. We'd conquered the second-ranked of the Five Highest. We stood 80 percent of the way home.

Only Mount Harvard barred our path to this stirring mountaineering accomplishment. Lamentably, Mount Harvard was cursed. For two years, work kept me away. Then Nathan had the temerity to move off for a job of his own, and he didn't seem enthralled with the idea of blowing limited vacation time to climb with me. He had grown remarkably impervious to guilt. Finally, in 2018, he briefly relented and we returned for Harvard, but freezing hail and sporadic bolts of lightning forced us off the mountain. Soon afterwards, the pandemic shut us in. It took till this past fall for the stars to align. We landed in Denver and drove to Leadville, at which point a witchcraft-induced medical affliction knocked me flat. The invaluable days we'd set aside for Harvard were lost.

The trip wasn't a total waste. Nathan climbed three peaks in the Mosquito Range with friends. We took a light hike up to an alpine lake as I recovered. But, in our Denver hotel room the night before flying home, sleep eluded me. The dream of the Five Highest Tops was slipping away. No rationalization about the folly of my mathematically grounded goals would erase the sting of its loss.

I kicked off the covers, rose and pulled back the drapes. Lights glistened icily from the city's skyscrapers and cranes. I had failed again, in multiple ways this time. I had promised I would curtail my invented quests, enter the wilderness more spiritually, and stop ringing up peaks like winnings on a slot machine, but here we were, enduring brutal flights, burning cash and vacation time, all while pursuing my selfish nonsense. Nathan surely couldn't give a rip about the Five Highest Tops, yet, with three a.m. darkness in my soul, I knew I'd disappointed him too. I'd dropped my end of the rope. My body was crumbling. Harvard, all fourteen miles and 4600 feet to climb, grew higher and more distant each passing year.

I turned away from the window. With his back to me, Nathan slept. Only a tousle of his dark hair showed above the blankets — but that glimpse felt hopeful somehow, resonating with just an ember of success. I had no right to take any credit. I'd just spent our mountaineering adventure flat on my back. I hadn't just sung my now-grown son to sleep. I never even worried if or how well he slept anymore. He wasn't that little boy, the one who had hiked so fearlessly into the mountains, any longer, yet I watched him sleep and felt an instinctive, undeniable victory. My child slept peacefully, and that knowledge filled me with warmth and relief. And in that moment, I finally realized our actual objective wasn't the Contiguous U.S. Five Highest Tops. It was the parent/child part of the equation.

Had I been a good father? I'd hesitate to ask. My guess is my fatherly performance approximates that of my checkered climbing career — great highs punctuated by numerous pratfalls and the rare flashing-light emergency. What's certain is that mountaineering has given me precious time with my son, times where we have moved in tandem, where we relied on one another's grace and judgment. The Five Highest Tops were a legacy, a frame constructed to hold memories of the days we were best together.

Harvard was still out there. It wasn't the Dawn Wall or North Face of the Eiger. Already a future expedition began forming in my mind, its outline indistinct as a ridge through fog. Nathan might protest, but already I felt intimations. I could have sworn I felt the jostling of the Forest Service road, heard the car doors' echoing slams, and strained for the trail sign's words under my headlamp's light.

Doug Emory is a freelance writer who lives just outside of Seattle. His range of publications is broad, including short stories and personal narratives that have appeared in highly regarded national magazines such as *Rock and Ice* and *Alpinist*. As an accomplished mountaineer, his writing often reflects his experiences in the mountains.

INSOMNIA

Mary Allen

I have fallen in love three times on my couch.

Thirty years ago Jim and I talked endlessly on my couch in my old apartment on Washington Street. We did that four nights in a row, and at the end of every night except the last one he stood up at midnight or one or one-thirty in the morning, said, *Thank you very much for another nice evening*, and walked back to his apartment up the street. When he said, *So, can I stay overnight?* on the fourth night I said no. No explanation or clarification, just no. I was too scared to say yes, and besides I had a stomachache and needed to get into my own bed alone. Later he said that worried him — was I not interested in him that way or what? We got that question straightened out the next night.

I fell in love with Marek on a different couch in a different house, the house I bought on Sheridan Avenue with the money I got for the book I wrote about Jim, who had long ago gone to the rooms of heaven by the time I was sitting on the new couch in the new house with Marek. Marek was someone so different from anyone or anything in my life, he might have been set down in my living room from Mars, although really he came from Fairfield, a town an hour and fifteen minutes away, where transcendental meditators meditate in a golden dome twice a day. Marek and I were sitting on a pale-green twill couch with tan piping in my Sheridan Avenue living room; he was telling me about his life, his divorce, his kids — they had small hamster-like pets called degus. "Little rat-like creatures," he said in his rolling Czech accent, and some penny dropped inside me, and I was suddenly in love with him. It didn't take long for me to be all in it after that, moving to Fairfield, having what was probably the first real sustained relationship with a man of my life.

I was sitting alone on my couch with my laptop on my lap, propped up against two large pillows, sipping a little glass of sherry, talking endlessly to a guy from Madison, when I fell in love the third time. I had gotten comfortable talking to people on Zoom during the pandemic, and I was especially comfortable talking to the guy from Madison.

The first time we talked I was sitting at my kitchen table, staring at his face on my laptop, on a Saturday afternoon. The next week we had another Zoom talk, two hours going on and on about this and that, warmly, comfortably, jokingly and teasingly, me first sitting at my kitchen table and then lying on my couch holding the laptop by my chest, because he said, *Why don't you get more comfortable somewhere*, because I was so tired from being awake from one-thirty a.m. to seven-thirty a.m. the night before. I was having early morning insomnia almost every night then, waking up at two or three or four, or sometimes even one in the morning, and lying awake in bed for hours. But I couldn't stop talking to him, didn't want to stop talking to him, even on top of all that exhaustion.

I kept getting messages from the dating app after I met him. One day I got one that said, *See who likes your profile*! I opened it up and saw a message from a guy named Phil who lived in Cedar Rapids, much closer to where I live than Madison, and he was a part-time journalist. He'd even published a piece in the same journal where I'd published something. *We have a lot in common*, his message said, *and I would like to meet you*. His photo hovered on the screen as if from above, gray hair, beard. The sight of it made me nauseous. Then I looked at the left side of the screen. There was a vertical row of small photos showing all the men I'd corresponded with on the dating app since I joined however long ago: A nice-looking guy named Thomas from Cedar Rapids that I had coffee with, whom I thought I might date until he sent me an unfriendly text message; a guy named Bobby from somewhere near Madison, who came down here to go a concert, met up with me, and went for a walk before the concert; he complained about everything — his hotel room, a dog snarling at another passing dog on the pedestrian mall, people who are gluten free when I told him that I didn't want half of his sandwich because I was gluten free. There was the plumber; the guy who lived on a farm with chickens and a poodle named Andrea; the retired pipefitter who had six parrots. I was charmed by those parrots, which had been acquired by the pipefitter's long-time girlfriend who'd died of cancer, but we never met and had nothing in common. All of those guys seemed intimidated, confused, and slightly frightened by the fact that I was a writer, as if I was a member of some alien species. I felt like a member of an alien species among them.

"Where can I read some of your writing?" M said the first time we made contact, on the dating app. I had seen his picture when I was trolling through my matches and went past it for some reason, didn't even look too closely at his profile. I told him I had written a memoir and he looked it up and ordered it from Amazon and in the meantime read some of the writing I had links to on my website. And we started corresponding.

You had me at *where can I read your writing*, I imagined saying to him later.

Nobody else I corresponded with on the dating app ever came close to getting the part of me that's a writer. But now there's this Phil who lives in Cedar Rapids, he understands being a writer, he is a writer, but the sight of him makes me sick. And then, in the line-up of small photos on the side of the screen — the pictures of all the men I've corresponded with on the dating app — I see the picture of the guy from Madison. And I feel something, it's almost as if I see something — light, warmth, happiness — shining through the photo, as if that photo is some portal to the future, to who knows what.

I'm standing at my bathroom sink reaching for my contact lens case on the shelf below the medicine cabinet when it happens. Somehow I nudge the little silver ring sitting on the shelf where I put it before I got into the shower and clink clink clink the little silver ring disappears down the sink drain. *Oh no*! I say loudly.

I try to raise the stopper to get it out but the stopper won't come out. I find the foot-long plastic wand with little backward spikes that Marek gave me years ago to fish hair out of the drain and stick that down the sink — no luck. I feel my distress rising.

"The ring isn't worth that much," M tells me when I call him to see if he can help me. "You haven't even had it for very long."

"That doesn't matter," I say in something approaching a wail. "It's the sentimental value."

He laughs and tells me what to do: Look under the sink and see if there's a metal strip attached to a blah blah blah and see if you can detach it. I lie down on the floor under the sink and try to do what he tells me, but the metal strip is attached to a screw that won't budge. He looks up a YouTube video and tells me patiently what the YouTube guy's directions are, but nothing I do works and we give up. I call the plumber, who comes over at twelve-thirty, takes the sink apart and fishes the ring out of the trap. "You might want to wash it off," he says, handing it to me in the kitchen. I rinse the ring under the kitchen faucet and put it back on my lefthand little finger. And then I breathe a sigh of relief.

We were sitting on my couch when he gave me the ring. It was the first time he came down here from Madison. I was telling him about my childhood, my terror of my mother, my living with a foster family because of it, my awful loud hyperventilating crying whenever my mother tried to make me live at home, and he said, "Just a minute, I have something to give you." He got up and rummaged around in his backpack and came back with a small midnight-blue velvet pouch. Inside was a tiny plastic bag with a little silver ring in it. An Irish friendship ring, with an open band and a little hand on each end of the band so it looks like the ring is hugging your finger when you wear it.

He didn't say anything when he handed it to me, but I knew what he was saying: This is so you'll feel held. Not really by me. Just held. Supported. At all times.

It looked way too small for me, but it slid easily onto my baby finger and I've been wearing it ever since. And I do feel held, by that ring, by *him*.

He stayed in a hotel during that first visit and there wasn't any touching. I didn't know if there was ever going to be any touching. During the second visit, when I went to Madison, there was cramming in side by side on his love seat. Lots of cramming in side by side. And late at night, after we had drunk most of a bottle of wine, passing the glass back and forth because he was in the middle of moving and he only had a single plastic wine glass so far in his new apartment, we were sitting there on the love seat and I was telling him about my insomnia. How I was still waking up at two or three or four or even. God forbid, one in the morning almost every night and lying awake for hours. I would be doing that soon in my hotel room about five minutes away from his apartment, where he would be taking me in about forty-five minutes. But right now we're still on the couch, and he says, "I really want to help you with your insomnia." He looks at me for a minute and then says, "I have an idea." He tells me to turn my back to him on the couch and he puts his arms around me from behind, all the way around, around my shoulders and arms, and stays that way for a good long minute while we listen to music, something by Phoebe Snow. And then he says, "Try to remember this when you're trying to go to sleep. This is how you should feel when you're falling asleep."

That's how I end up on the daybed with him. It's the end of the night during his second visit to Iowa City. A while ago we went out to his car in the cool moist one-a.m. air to collect his sleeping bag — *I'll sleep in your den on my sleeping bag*, he said when we were making our plans about him coming down this time. *I have blankets!* I said. *I didn't want you to have to wash your bedding just because I stayed at your house*, he said when he got here.

He rolls his sleeping bag out on the daybed now, lies down on the bed and holds out his arms. *Come here, I'll help you fall asleep*, he says.

I'm not going to go to sleep if I get into that bed with you! I say. But I get into the bed with him anyway, of course I do, and he encourages me to turn on my side with my back to him and he puts his arms around me, all the way around, just like on his love seat in Madison, and I feel enclosed, safe, held in a way I have never been held in my life.

Somehow we start whispering, although there's no one in the house to wake up with our talking, no one to hear us except my cats. *Is virtual hugging better*, he whispers in a doubting voice, as if I would actually say that I would fall asleep more easily if he was hugging me in some virtual way that didn't involve arms and bodies and warmth, as if I could possibly not like doing this.

No, I whisper.

Maybe you could use a lullaby, he said last week, still trying to come up with something that would help me sleep all the way through the night. *Would a lullaby help?*

Yes, I said. We were on the phone, him in Madison and me in Iowa City like usual. *I would love that.* So he recorded himself playing the guitar and singing "Sweet Baby James" and put the recording on a YouTube channel where you can find him playing guitar and singing other songs. *This is for anyone who could use a lullaby*, he said to introduce it, smiling a little smile that let me know he was thinking of me. I watched it in my bed at night, twice, grinning broadly. It did not put me to sleep.

Now, on the daybed, he whispers the lyrics to that song, not singing but speaking them to the back of my head. *There is a young cowboy, he lives on the range. His horse and his cattle are his only companions.*

That's the nicest thing anyone has ever said to me, I say when he's finished, and then I sit up, turn around, lean over, and kiss him. I don't even hesitate. First I kiss him on the top of his arm, then I kiss him on the lips, just a small almost-closed-mouth buss. He looks a little startled as I lower my face to his.

Then I go in my room and get into my own bed. The first thing I think when I wake up at five-thirty in the morning is how awful it will be if I go into the den and he's not here. What if he went home in the middle of the night? But he didn't go home in the middle of the night. He's awake and I go in there and he pulls the sleeping bag back and I get back into bed with him.

Mary Allen is the author of a literary memoir, *The Rooms of Heaven*, published by Alfred A. Knopf and Vintage Books, and a collection of personal essays, *The Deep Limitless Air: A Memoir in Pieces*, published by Bluelight Press. She is a recipient of an NEA grant for creative writing. She has a regular blog on the *Psychology Today* website and has also published short work in

Poets & Writers, Real Simple, Library Journal, CNN On-line, Shenandoah, Tiferet Journal, The Chaos, and *Beloit Fiction Review.* She received an MFA from the Iowa Writers' Workshop and teaches in the University of Iowa's Summer Writing Festival, making .her living as a full-time writing coach.